THE
MAN
WHO
INVENTED
SATURDAY
MORNING

THE
MAN
WHO
INVENTED
SATURDAY
MORNING

AND
OTHER
ADVENTURES
IN
AMERICAN
ENTERPRISE

DAVID
OWEN

VILLARD BOOKS
NEW YORK  1988

For Mom and Dad

Library of Congress Cataloging-in-Publication Data

Owen, David, 1955-
The man who invented Saturday morning.

1. Laissez-faire — Anecdotes, facetiae, satire, etc.
2. Laissez-faire — History.   I. Title.
HB95.094   1988   330.12′2   87-29660
ISBN 0-394-56810-9

Manufactured in the United States of America

23456789

First edition

Book design by Elizabeth Frenchman

ACKNOWLEDGMENTS

*T*he first four essays in this book were originally published in *Harper's;* the others appeared first in *The Atlantic.* I've fiddled with all of them since then.

Special thanks to William Whitworth, Corby Kummer, Deborah McGill, Jack Beatty, Cullen Murphy, and everyone else at *The Atlantic;* to Michael Kinsley, Helen Rogan, and all the others from the brief Golden Age of *Harper's;* to Ann Hodgman, my wife and editor-in-chief; to Julia Coopersmith, my agent; to Diane Reverand, my editor at Villard; and to Aunt Gail Culver, who suggested writing about cadavers.

CONTENTS

THE MAN WHO INVENTED SATURDAY MORNING

I.
THE SOUL
OF A NEW DESSERT

---

*F*or breakfast this morning I started off with a carton of Fresh 'N Frosty. Fresh 'N Frosty is sort of a cross between a ballpark frosty malt and a McDonald's milk shake. The one I had was chocolate-flavored. Then, after coffee, I had three strawberries, a couple of blueberries, a boysenberry, a peach slice, and some loganberry puree. Then I had a piece of devil's food cream cake. Then about four bites each from brand-new cartons of chocolate, vanilla, and strawberry Fresh 'N Frosty.

I was getting a little thirsty now, so I had a glass of water and a vanilla milk shake. Then I had a spoonful of tartar sauce. There was no fish to go with the tartar sauce, but to tell you the truth, I've never been a big fan of fish for breakfast. Then half of a Bavarian cream-filled chocolate éclair. Then all of a chocolate cream puff. A glass of apple juice. A slice of strawberry shortcake. And, finally, a little pie-in-a-plastic-cup concoction that had a layer of cookie crumbs, a layer of minty filling, and a layer of creamy topping. I could have eaten more, but it was almost time for lunch.

My host for breakfast this morning was Rich Products Corporation, a food manufacturing company in Buffalo, New York. Rich's best-known product is Coffee Rich, the stuff you put in coffee. For more than an hour, while birds were chirping in the trees, I sat on a stool in one of Rich's test kitchens and sampled a huge variety of treats.

The most remarkable thing about the food I ate was not its quantity but its temperature: everything I put in my mouth was frozen. The strawberry shortcake I ate was at minus 22 degrees Fahrenheit. That's ten degrees colder than Fairbanks in January and exactly the same temperature as the surface of Mars. I took a bite, chewed it up, and swallowed it right down. The pieces of fruit were at about 8 degrees. The chocolate éclair was served directly from the freezer.

Ice is warmer than what I ate; it's also harder. Ordinary frozen strawberries are so hard they bounce like billiard balls when you throw them against the wall. Let them thaw for a couple of hours and they collapse into puddles of watery red mush. But Rich's frozen strawberries are soft and sweet and firm at temperatures far below freezing. I plunked them into my mouth and chewed them up. Chewing them didn't hurt my fillings; swallowing them didn't hurt my throat.

You may think it's easy to keep food soft at 5 degrees Fahrenheit. All you have to do, you'll say, is load it up with a lot of chemicals—like antifreeze. But the process that Rich has invented doesn't involve the addition of chemicals. The frozen tartar sauce I tried contained vegetable oil, corn syrup, pickled cucumbers, vinegar, pickled onions, salt, sugar, citric acid, vegetable gum, mustard powder, and spices. Yet even at zero degrees Fahrenheit it could be spooned right out of a jar and into my mouth. The onions were crisp and tasty. The pickles were firm and pickly.

Rich's new freezing process—which is called Freeze Flo—does more than merely keep foods soft. It also keeps them from getting soggy. If you accidentally leave one of Rich's frozen éclairs sitting on your kitchen counter after dinner Friday night, the pastry shell will still be dry and flaky on Tuesday morning. And after three days at room temperature, the éclair will still be safe to eat: Rich's new frozen foods do not support bacterial growth. A researcher at the company once injected thousands of bacterial colonies into the filling of a chocolate éclair. After several days at room temperature, all the bacteria were dead. Freeze Flo products can be repeatedly thawed and refrozen, which means they are cheaper to transport and store. In fact, some Freeze Flo products don't really need to be frozen at all.

It isn't hard to imagine applications for Freeze Flo foods. How about strawberry ice cream with whole, soft strawberries in it? Or frozen pies you can eat directly out of (or inside) your freezer? Or frozen juice concentrates you can pour and mix without thawing? Or hot dogs you can store for six months in your kitchen cabinet (yuck)? Or a chocolate éclair you can eat half of and then refreeze?

Rich's is already making some of these products; others are being licensed to independent manufacturers. In all, the company holds about forty patents in this country and abroad. New uses for the process are being discovered all the time. Freeze Flo, according to an article in *The Frozen Food Executive* (published by the National Frozen Food Association, "Voice of the frozen food industry"), "may turn out to be the most revolutionary development in frozen foods since Clarence Birdseye froze his first fish."

Freeze Flo may turn out to be a revolutionary development in other areas as well. "Food chemistry and medical chemistry have a lot in common," says a Rich Products executive. Company scientists are now working hard on secret experiments they refuse to discuss in public. Patents have been applied for. An announcement will be forthcoming. Freeze Flo may even prove to be the long-awaited cure for—

But I'm getting ahead of myself.

*L*ong ago, many thousands of years before the invention of Freeze Flo, primitive man "ate what he wanted, then left the rest," according to a Rich Products promotional film. This was pretty dumb, considering primitive man's habit of starving to death. But eventually he learned about salting, smoking, and spicing his leftovers. "Each method preserved the food, but changed it in some way." A few more years passed. Then, up north, primitive man discovered that he could preserve foods by packing them in snow and ice. "True, thawing took time." But thawed foods tasted good, and, as the centuries flew by and human civilization advanced in ways far too numerous to describe in a single sentence, "frozen food technology improved."

At long last, in 1929, Clarence Birdseye froze his epochal fish, and the modern age of frozen food began. Well, actually, food had been frozen commercially before 1929. In 1869, for example, pigeons were frozen and sold in some parts of the United States. But this was mere child's play compared with what Birdseye accomplished at the dawn of the Great Depression. His major contributions, according to one authority on extremely cold food, had to do with "selection, handling, preparation, freezing, storage, transportation, and marketing"—in short, everything. He was also the first important freezer of vegetables. (The most frequently frozen vegetable in the world is the pea.)

One of the most interesting facts about the frozen food industry, I think, is that the Birds Eye Company (today a division of General Foods) was named after an actual person (though General Foods, of course, was not). I had no idea. If you think about it, though, it makes perfect sense: Why would anyone name a frozen food company after the eye of a bird? (Fish's Eye, on the other hand, would have a certain logic to it, because the eyes of fish played an important, though little-known, role in the early years of the industry. In 1899, in a report published by the United States Fish Commission, a man named C. H. Stevenson put his finger on the major obstacle facing would-be freezers of fish: "the eye dries up and loses its shining appearance after a long exposure to cold.")

Clarence Birdseye's estimable achievements notwithstanding, the early history of frozen food was not an unbroken chain of triumphs. Three decades before he was elected president, Richard Nixon tried to manufacture a frozen orange-juice product called Citra-Frost. Frozen orange juice turned out to be a good idea, but Nixon froze his in plastic bags, which were continually breaking. Humiliated by the fickle goddess of subfreezing temperatures, the young man from Whittier turned his attention to politics.

Still, there were plenty of exhilarating moments. In 1942, 61,566 pounds of succotash were frozen in the United States. One year later, the territory of Alaska boasted 1,293,000 cubic feet of refrigerated storage space. Other milestones were passed in due course. By 1950, in their book *The Freezing Preparation of Foods*, Donald K. Tressler and Clifford F. Evers felt justified in predicting that even chillier days were ahead. "When nearly all kitchens have equipment for freezing and storing perishable foods," they prophesied tautologically, "the use of frozen foods will be well-nigh universal."

*P*aul and Eleanor Rich of Buffalo, New York, brought five children into the world, but only one of them—Bob—grew up to make a major contribution to the frozen food industry. Robert E. Rich, the future founder and chairman of Rich Products Corporation, was born on July 7, 1913, sixteen years before the official invention of frozen food. His father was a dairyman who switched to the ice cream business after discovering he couldn't stand to sell milk.

Growing up in the Rich household was considered quite the thing in early twentieth-century Buffalo. "Everyone loved to go to the Riches," a neighbor later recalled, "because refreshments were superior." Paul Rich brought home a different flavor of ice cream every night. He also allowed his children to play football in a cemetery and to wrestle, on mats that he himself provided, in a garage. "I think wrestling is the finest sport there is," Bob Rich says today. Every winter, when the citizens of Buffalo were too cold to buy ice cream, Paul Rich moved his family to Palm Beach.

When Bob graduated from the University of Buffalo— where he had been captain of the football team and founder, captain, and coach of the wrestling team, and where he would one day be inducted into the athletic hall of fame—his father gave him $5,000. Bob used the money to make a down payment on a dairy. He disliked the milk business as intensely as his father did, but he wanted to assert his independence. To keep his sanity, he moonlighted as a football coach. His first appointment was at Riverside High School, whose team had often finished lower, but never higher, than next to last. In his first year as coach, the team finished seventh. In his second year, it was undefeated. "EYES OF BUFFALO ARE FOCUSED ON BOB RICH'S CREW" was the headline in a local newspaper the day before Riverside won the city championship.

During the Second World War, Rich worked for the War Production Board and was appointed milk administrator for the state of Michigan. His job was to divert excess milk to thirsty American soldiers. One day he paid a visit to the George Washington Carver Laboratory, a research institution endowed by Henry Ford. The laboratory's principal activity was supplying Detroit's Ford Hospital with a product Rich had never seen before: milk made from soybeans.

In a certain sense, Henry Ford's career can be viewed as a plot to eradicate large domestic animals. Having rendered the horse obsolete with his automobile, he had now set out to eliminate the cow. Carver scientists spent their days striving to realize their benefactor's vision of a cattle-free society. Periodically Ford threw parties for journalists at which he served nothing but milk, ice cream, hamburgers, cheese, and other foods made from soybeans. (Who but a journalist would attend such a party?) He also built a soybean car.

Ford's antagonism toward cows struck a chord in Robert E. Rich. Rich, after all, was a second-generation hater of the dairy business.

"I'd always said that the cow was the most inefficient manufacturing plant in America," he says today. "Its product is eighty-seven percent water, and it's high in bacteria, and it has to be pasteurized. A cow will go out and step on its udder and develop mastitis. It will eat leeks, which makes it milk taste like onions. I've seen cows that have waddled. They were drunk on silage. The color of cow's milk changes at different times of the year, and the taste changes. You hear people talk about 'pure cream,' but that's laughable. There's no such thing. You can say 'pure vegetable oil,' though, because there you just don't run into all the problems you do with a cow."

Rich went back to Buffalo immediately and, with the help of a chemist he knew, figured out a way to make his own soybean milk. "It seemed to me that if we could get it into a whipped cream," Rich says, "then we'd have a better product than the cow's product, and the price would be lower." In November of 1944 he founded Rich Products Corporation to manufacture his invention, converting his dairy's garage into the production plant for the world's first nondairy whipped topping. Its name: Whip Topping.

At first, Rich distributed Whip Topping to the customers on his milk routes, billing it variously as "The Miracle Cream from the Soybean" and "Gold from the Soil." The early months were not a fabulous success. "We were not chemists," an employee later admitted. But gradually Rich refined his formula, and in 1946 he was invited to make a sales presentation to a refrigerated-food distributor on Long Island. He packed some samples in dry ice and newspaper and took the overnight train to New York.

The following morning, while fifty salesmen looked on, Rich took out his samples and discovered with horror that they had frozen solid. He began to perspire. Cow's cream, he knew, would not whip after freezing. "I thought briefly about telling them I had brought them all together to unveil a great way to keep newspapers cold." He stalled for as long as he could, then borrowed a knife and hacked nervously at his frozen soybean cream until he could fit the pieces into a mixing bowl. He held his breath. "It whipped to perfection."

No one was more surprised than Bob Rich. But he had the presence of mind to realize that he had done more than escape from a potentially embarrassing situation: He had invented the world's first *frozen* nondairy whipped topping. That meant that his market was no longer limited to Buffalo. Now he could sell Whip Topping anywhere in the world. He later whipped up a bowlful for Ben Strickenberg, the most powerful retail food distributor in New York. Strickenberg had a 103-degree fever at the time. "He tasted it and took another spoonful without saying anything," Bob Rich later reported. "He paced around the room three or four times and came back and pointed his finger in my face and said, 'Young man, you have a fortune in that bowl.'"

Quite by accident, Rich Products Corporation had entered the age of frozen food.

*R*ich's still sells Whip Topping, along with a wide range of other products: *Whipped* Topping, Sundi-Whip, bread dough, cake icing, pudding, pancake batter, jelly donuts, frozen shrimp, and cheesecake—not to mention the whole new Freeze Flo line, including Fresh 'N Frosty. Also, of course, Coffee Rich, the world's first frozen all-vegetable coffee creamer. When Coffee Rich was introduced, in the mid-1960s, the dairy industry spent hundreds of thousands of dollars trying to keep it off the market. Coffee Rich, they said, was "imitation cream," and hence against the law. But forty separate court decisions ruled in Rich's favor. In 1974 the Kansas Supreme Court declared that Coffee Rich was "a new and distinct food." Finally, the milk lobby gave up.

You may never consciously have bought a Rich product, but you almost certainly have eaten one. The company's wares are sold under dozens of independent labels (The Colonel's Chocolate Pudding, for example) and dispensed in enormous quantities by institutions and food services. If you've ever bought anything in the bakery at your grocery store, there's a fairly good chance you've bought something made by Rich. Likewise if you've ever drunk coffee or eaten dessert in a restaurant. All this adds up to a lot of business.

Rich Products Corporation is privately owned, so don't run out and try to buy a lot of stock options. Bob Rich is still the chairman of the board. His son, Bob Rich, Jr., is now president. The first year Bob Sr. was in business, the company had approximately $30,000 in sales. It now sells that much every ten minutes.

For $15,000 or so one day, I stood beside a machine that was making Coffee Rich. One part of the machine made the cartons, another part filled them with Coffee Rich, another part pinched them shut. It wasn't hard to understand why Bob Rich and Henry Ford used to think so little of cows: That machine really knew what it was doing.

I was touring Rich's main manufacturing plant, directly across the street from corporate headquarters. With me were two young women from public relations and a very enthusiastic man, our guide. We had entered the plant through an old, green house that was once the company's main office and, before that, the home of either Wells or Fargo (I don't remember which). I was dressed as I usually am on these occasions: jacket, tie, loafers, hair net. The last item is mandatory in the plant; our guide was wearing a hard hat over his.

After standing in a puddle and watching a machine make boxes for a while, we stepped into a dark room where the temperature was 20 degrees below zero. Instantly, my Bic pen stopped writing. Our guide said he had worked in there for thirteen years, and there was longing in his voice. Snow was falling from the ceiling. Cases of Rich products were piled up everywhere, like supplies for an Arctic expedition. The cold, to me, felt life-threatening. At last we entered a slightly warmer room filled with thirty-pound cans of chilled, pasteurized, liquid eggs. "We're going to make quiche tomorrow."

Our entourage moved on. Upstairs, in the mixing room, the air was thick with the smell of butterscotch—for my money, the world's most horrifying flavor. A man on a ladder was emptying hundred-pound bags of sugar into what appeared to be gigantic washing machine. The sugar came in the kind of bags you buy dog food and fertilizer in. There was a hose lying on the floor beside a sign that said HANG UP HOSE. Outside, at the loading dock, a tank truck was pumping liquid sugar into an opening in the ground.

Back downstairs, we arrived at the true object of our journey, the machine that makes Fresh 'N Frosty, the new Freeze Flo dessert. To my trained reportorial eye, the machine that makes Fresh 'N Frosty looked pretty much like the machine, just a few paces away, that makes Whip Topping. But of course the two machines are worlds apart. Whip Topping is the past, Fresh 'N Frosty is the future. Chocolatey goo (brown gold!) splurted out of a nozzle into a procession of twelve-ounce cups. Our guide reached over and grabbed a cup for each of us. Splurt, splurt, splurt. That's the new sound of frozen food.

"We've had opportunities to sell this business a thousand times over," Bob Jr. told me later on. "But we don't even entertain offers."

Bob Jr. started out in business the same way Bob Sr. did, with a bankroll provided by his father. In 1962, when he graduated from Williams—where he had been co-captain of the varsity hockey team—he thought he wanted to be either a jet pilot or a CIA agent. Then his father offered to put him in charge of a brand-new Rich's plant in Canada and give him a million-dollar budget to do with what he would. "I was convinced in college that my father knew very little at all and that I knew everything," Bob Jr. says. "Communication was nonexistent." Still, he took up his father's challenge. After a few Canadian catastrophes—the Whip Topping periodically failed to whip, among other things—he decided the old man was pretty smart after all. "Now he's my best friend," Bob Jr. says. "We have a great relationship."

Bob Jr. is tall and handsome and has his father's piercing blue eyes. His hair is long, curly, and brown. He looks like one of those Canadian hockey stars who are always opening restaurants in New York. He is forty-two years old, but his office has a number of pleasing little-boy touches: a couple of model airplanes, a little statue of a man on a horse (actually, it's a polo player), and some Charles Clough canvases that look like finger paintings. Almost everyone calls him Bob. All in all, Rich Products Corporation struck me as a fun place to work. In 1981, when Rich's celebrated its twenty-fifth anniversary, a worker in the production plant had the company logo tattooed on his arm.

Bob Jr. is a well-known nice guy, but he is also a shrewd businessman. After graduating first in his class from a special executive MBA program at the University of Rochester, he established the company's first marketing department and embarked on a bold program of acquisitions. One of his favorite purchases was a company called SeaPak, a shrimp processor owned by W. R. Grace & Co. Grace wanted out of the shrimp business, and the Coca-Cola Company was thinking about getting in. Swarms of Coke consultants descended on SeaPak and spent nine months poring over ledgers and rummaging through file cabinets. Finally the head of SeaPak became so exasperated that he called up Bob Jr. and said, "Why don't you buy us and get these Coke guys off our backs?" Bob Jr. and Sr. flew down the following day. They looked at the books over breakfast, retired to the men's room for a conference, washed their hands, returned to the table, bought the company, and went home.

The Riches' preference in corporate acquisitions is for father-and-son companies that face extinction because the fathers want to sell out and retire. The Bobs move in, inject new capital, and leave the sons in charge. The result is an uncommonly contented stable of acquirees and an unusually rosy outlook for the corporation as a whole. It was precisely one such acquisition that led to the discovery of Freeze Flo.

*M*arvin L. Kahn wouldn't have fit into the Rich household. He was a walking symposium of childhood diseases: mumps, chicken pox, measles, polio. Born into a poor Brooklyn family in 1935, he wrestled with his invisible demons and dreamed of a career in science. His father, a stern German immigrant, moved from bad job to worse job, taking his family first to Massachusetts, then to New Jersey. Kahn yearned for a better life. He worked hard in high school and won a full scholarship to New York University's College of Engineering. Someday, he hoped, he would have his own laboratory at a company like Standard Oil.

Kahn's dream evaporated when his uncle, who had started a wholesale bakery business with his father, suddenly died. Kahn was forced to switch to night school and spend his days unloading trucks at his father's plant. Then, in 1967, the elder Kahn fell ill and dropped the company in Marvin's lap. "He said, 'All right, now *you* run the business, wise college kid.' " The company was deeply in debt. Marvin's knowledge of management didn't extend beyond the loading dock.

Still, the young man had some new ideas he wanted to try. During his decade as a laborer he had passed the time by creating new products in the only laboratory to which he had access: his mind. What would happen, Kahn wondered, if a baker didn't have to make everything from scratch? What if, instead of making his icing every morning before dawn, he could simply open a can?

"All of a sudden," Kahn says today, "I started to think, maybe I can save this business." He formulated an icing that remained stable in a can and took it to a Dunkin' Donuts convention. He came away with $1.2 million in orders. "That was six times the business we had ever had," Kahn says today. "The company was profitable from there on out."

Kahn rapidly expanded his company's line, adding fillings, glazes, and fruits. In 1973, the Bobs, who with their frozen batters and doughs had been moving in a similar direction, bought the company. Kahn was put in charge of research and development for Rich Products Corporation. After many years of waiting, he finally had his lab.

He also had another idea. "At that time," he says today, "the Achilles heel of the industry, as I saw it, was that most in-store bakeries didn't have enough refrigerated shelf space. As a result, they were offering only a rather mediocre line of doughnuts, sweet rolls, breads, and sometimes pies, but none of the fancier cakes that complete a bakery's product line. And I thought that perhaps we could come up with a filling and an icing that would supply the answer by staying fresh without refrigeration."

But bacteria thrive on unrefrigerated icings, causing them to spoil very quickly. One way to preserve a food is to dry it, eliminating the water that bacteria need to live. Drying was clearly impractical for an icing, Kahn knew, but maybe there was another solution. Maybe it would be possible simply to *hide* the water—to bind it chemically to the other ingredients. He made a topping using the method he had conceived and left it sitting at room temperature for two months. "It didn't spoil, and it didn't dry, and it didn't crack." He paid a visit to the Bobs.

"Marvin came in to see us," Bob Jr. says, "and told us that he'd developed a topping that was better than our whipped topping and didn't require refrigeration. Well, this was like calling your child a bad name. But we said we'd take a look. So he brought in a sample, and it looked good, the color was nice, it whipped up well, and everything was fine. Except that it tasted *just awful*. Like concrete."

The Bobs politely suggested that Kahn stick his topping

in the freezer for a while, on the chance that exposure to intense cold might change the taste—something that often happens with frozen foods. Kahn did as he was told and then, disappointed, went home for the weekend.

When he checked his sample again on Monday, he was surprised to find that it was still soft. The freezer must have broken down, he decided. All of Rich's freezers have recording thermometers in them, so a technician was dispatched to check the readout. He returned with a strange discovery: the freezer's temperature hadn't risen above 40 degrees below zero all weekend long. Now Kahn was genuinely puzzled. He inserted a thermometer into his topping and watched in astonishment as the mercury fell slowly to minus 20 degrees.

Gradually Kahn began to realize what must have happened. If you bind up the water in a product, you do more than eliminate a medium for bacteria: you make it impossible for ice crystals to form. And ice crystals are what make frozen food hard. Entirely by accident, Kahn had discovered a way to make a frozen food that didn't have to be thawed.

"It's quite ironic," Bob Jr. says, "that we got started in this business by having a product turn hard that we wanted to stay soft, and now we've secured our future by having a product stay soft that we wanted to get hard."

"A plant, as it grows, takes nutrients from the soil," Marvin Kahn told me in one of his rare free moments. "We learned this in regular high school chemistry, maybe even in a grammar school science course. The nutrients are all dissolved in water in the soil; the trick is to get the water up through the root to the flower or the leaf or the stem. There are no miniature pumps in a plant. The way it gets those nutrients is through a phenomenon called osmosis, which has to do with the equalization of fluid concentrations on both sides of a permeable membrane.

"In Freeze Flo, we do it just the same way. Knowing the differential in pressures in, for example, a strawberry, we can take the free water out of the berry and put in water that has been bound to fructose or to other natural sugars in the fruit. We replace free water with bound water. In formulated products like fillings, we simply make changes in the ingredients."

"That sounds pretty simple," I said (lying). "Why didn't anybody think of it before?"

"I don't know," Kahn said. "For example, in the dried-fruit area, we don't know why we're coming up with dried fruits that make ordinary raisins and dried apricots look like nothing. We just don't understand why no one else has done it."

Kahn went back to his office to get some samples. He returned with plastic containers of dried grapes, dried blueberries, and dried apricots. He had made them by submitting fresh fruits to the Freeze Flo process, then removing some of the water. "There's nothing added to those," he said as I sampled a big, golden, delicious Freeze Flo raisin. "Ordinary raisins have sulfur dioxide and other chemicals added to them to prevent them from rotting. Some dried fruits are loaded up with sulfur to keep them from discoloring. We don't do any of those things. These, when placed in cereal, plumb back up their natural shape and give off sweetness to the cereal, which means the cereal doesn't have to be presweetened."

Kahn and his assistants have come up with so many applications for Freeze Flo that Rich has begun licensing other companies to manufacture its inventions. Freeze Flo is already popular in Europe, where refrigeration equipment is much less common than it is in the United States. On the day I spoke with Kahn, representatives from companies in Germany, Sweden, and the Netherlands were wandering around the hallways.

Freeze Flo has been slower to gain acceptance in this country. There are several reasons. One of them, Kahn says, is NIH—Not Invented Here syndrome. American businessmen, much more than European businessmen, tend to pooh-pooh ideas they didn't think up all by themselves. When Kahn and a couple of other Rich's executives went to make a licensing presentation at a large consumer-products company whose name you would recognize immediately, the research-and-development people in the audience were fidgety and unimpressed. "Their attitude was, 'We've got twenty-three hundred people in R and D and you've only got forty. How could you come up with better things that we can come up with?' At one point a company scientist stood up and said, 'We learned all this in high school chemistry, and we've done this before, and this is nothing new.' There was a silence. Finally someone else stood up and said, 'That's what they said about Pampers.' "

*K*ahn told me he had to rush off somewhere, but before he did I asked him if it was true, as I had heard, that he was experimenting with medical applications for Freeze Flo.

"Yes, I am," he said. "But I can't talk about it. We have a very exciting breakthrough that I think we'll be able to announce very soon. We've got to get the patents first, though."

"Does it involve freezing tissues?" I asked. One of the big problems with freezing parts of people is that the water inside cells expands, destroying the cells. Sounds like a job for Freeze Flo.

"Let's just say it involves freezing living organisms in the body."

"And cancer cells?"

I expected Kahn to laugh at this. But he said, "It's possible. . . ." The project he's been working on has nothing to do with cancer—"I would be misleading you if I led you to think that"—but I could tell by the tone of his voice that, forty patents later, Marvin Kahn had stopped being surprised by the uses for his invention.

If you're the sort of American who pays no attention to things that other people invent, then you'd just better watch your step. Freeze Flo is going to change your life whether you like it or not. You may not eat Fresh 'N Frosty for breakfast—and I may never eat it again—but someday, somewhere, your life will be made perhaps as much as 1 percent more convenient as a result of what Rich Products Corporation has done.

And who knows? Someday, twenty or thirty years from now, our children may look back in wonder at that astonishing day in Buffalo, when the topping that tasted terrible was put in the freezer but didn't get hard, and exclaim, as with a single voice, "Now, *that* was the true and immortal dawn of the Golden Age of Frozen Food!"

(1983)

"**Y**ou need to take the time to touch and smell a baby's head," says Tom Sullivan, the lunchtime speaker. He is addressing an overflowing crowd in the Grand Ballroom of Stouffer's Riverfront Towers in St. Louis. The occasion is the annual convention of Meeting Planners International (MPI), an association of people who make their livings planning meetings and conventions. A meeting of professional meeting planners is one of those rare and wonderful phenomena—like the alignment of all nine planets on the same side of the sun—that tingle with cosmic portent.

Tom Sullivan's topic is "You Are Special." He's pretty special himself. Blind since birth, he is an avid golfer who once beat Jack Nicklaus by three strokes in an exhibition. He rowed in the Henley Regatta and tried out for the 1968 U.S. Olympic wrestling team. He has made thirty-seven skydives. He says he earned a degree in clinical psychology at Harvard (he didn't really). He has appeared on *Mork and Mindy*. He has arranged songs for Sammy Davis, Jr. Today he is a special correspondent for *Good Morning America* and a popular convention speaker.

"I want to come here today," he says, "to pay tribute to the most misunderstood and abused group of human beings on earth." He is referring not to people who can't see but to people who plan meetings. "I think that my experience with meeting planners has made me realize that, frankly, you're the best of life."

Standing on the podium, his seeing-eye dog beside him, Sullivan says, "I need to share something with you, because you need to understand that I made a turning point." His voice cracking, he describes a day nine years ago. His wife had gone shopping. His four-year-old daughter wanted to be taken for a swim in the family pool. A young woman sitting near me begins, already, to weep.

"The telephone rang," Sullivan continues, himself teetering on the verge of tears, "and it was my first major record offer." Pause. "And I wasn't paying attention to the little girl." Long pause. "And ladies and gentlemen, that happens to all of us." He is whispering into the microphone now. "Whether you're in the hotel business, the airline business, or you plan meetings—" he pauses again, takes a deep breath, and then nearly screams: "YOU ARE IN THE *PEOPLE* BUSINESS!" The room is echoing. "And I know that better than anyone else, because I'm called 'disabled.' What a lot of *crap* that is. You're in the people business. And so, while I was on the phone, you see, the little girl fell in the swimming pool."

Sullivan has told this story many times at many conventions. A number of people sitting in this room have heard it before, some of them more than once. But Sullivan makes it sound fresh every time. His voice, at this point, is a sort of whispered sob.

"And I dove into the pool," he says, "and I scrambled around . . . and then there was a quiet sound. *You* wouldn't hear it, not because you couldn't, just because you wouldn't. It was the sound of her air bubbles, and they blipped, blipped, blipped their way to the surface."

Sullivan followed the sound, found his daughter, and resuscitated her. Today she is in excellent health. The accident was a terrifying moment that changed Sullivan's life and taught him an enduring lesson about the convention industry. "I started to realize the relevance of what counts in this life," he says. "You see, ladies and gentlemen, you get hung up in tasks that are critical to other people but that seem menial to you."

It's almost time to start serving the food, so Sullivan draws his remarks to a close. "The process of human evolution," he concludes, "can only occur if you celebrate your own uniqueness. The bottom line of my being here, frankly, is that that's why I've come: to be part of the celebration of your— *your*—very, very special uniqueness. Have a good lunch everybody!"

And with that he puts one hand on the harness of his seeing-eye dog and the other hand on the shoulder of a man in a sport coat, and the three of them go running around the perimeter of the Grand Ballroom, and they disappear through the door. Lunch is served.

*M*eeting planners plan meetings, which are small conventions held by corporations. Sometimes they plan conventions, which are large meetings held by associations. Associations also have meetings and corporations also have conventions. Conventions are often referred to as meetings and meetings are sometimes referred to as conventions. Of course, meeting planners plan their own conventions, including this one, which they call a conference. (In Europe, conventions are usually known as congresses.)

Whatever you call them, conventions are an American institution, a very big business, and an important part of our country's very special uniqueness. The United States, as several meeting planners reminded me, was founded at a convention. In 1981, according to the International Association of Convention and Visitors Bureaus, something like eighty-seven thousand conventions were held in the United States. Roughly $16 billion was spent by the forty-seven million people who held and attended them. Convention attendees (this is the term everybody uses, although of course at any given convention there is only one attendee, the convention itself, while the people in attendance are attenders) account for an additional $5 billion or so in airplane tickets.

Given the size of the market, it's hardly surprising that lots of different people should be trying to grab a share of it. More than a dozen American cities are now building new convention centers or expanding old ones. Brand-new convention hotels are being built as fast as architects can design them and developers can give them names like Cloister Plantation House and Breckenridge Concourse.

One city that's working especially hard to attract convention business is The Meeting Place. When I was growing up in Kansas City, on the other side of the state, The Meeting Place was known as St. Louis. Not anymore. The name was

changed by the Convention and Visitors Bureau in order to
stress the city's new commitment to conventions. Attracting
Meeting Planners International was thus an enormous coup.
So was attracting the Miss Universe pageant, which was being
held in the city at exactly the same time, a fact I discovered
too late to do me any good.

Before Miss Universe came to town, St. Louis's biggest
selling point, conventionwise, had been the fact that it's not
much farther from anywhere than it is from everywhere else.
According to the convention bureau, nearly 90 million people
could hop in their cars right now, drive no more than all day
long, and be there. Although there aren't all that many people
in St. Louis to begin with, virtually everyone can get there
by flying for about two hours. "There's no better place than
St. Louis for meeting people halfway," says a Meeting Place
advertisement the city bought in a trade magazine last year.
Another ad showed a picture of Marlin Perkins holding a
chimpanzee. "Come to St. Louis," the headline said. "We'll
greet you in style." Among the city's many attractions, according to another ad, is "a veritable United Nations of fine
restaurants." The city also has a big convention center, completed in 1977, that is named after former mayor Alphonso J.
Cervantes.

*C*ities like conventions because people like conventions.
There's no denying that they are fun to go to. For one thing,
most people come home from them with a lot of free stuff. I
left the MPI convention with: a little plaque that says CATCH
THE SPIRIT OF ST. LOUIS; three bottles of beer, all presented
to me (not in person) by Anheuser-Busch Companies; a glass

to drink my beer from; a T-shirt; a little bar of Tone soap, courtesy of my hotel; a thing of shampoo; a St. Louis Cardinals visor; a towel with certain information about the convention printed on it; a book of photographs of Missouri; three sweat-bands; my name tag; and many other items too numerous to mention. On the airplane back to New York I saw some of my fellow conventioneers admiring their brand-new ruler-clock-calculators, which had the word Ramada printed on them. Seeing those fancy rulers almost ruined my trip. Why didn't I get one? Was it because I skipped the closing luncheon? But I got over it before we landed.

Conventions try to be serious as well. As an MPI official said just before the opening session, "The byword of MPI is education." MPI has more than 5,600 members. This year's conference gave roughly 1,400 of them a chance to share ideas about meetings and conventions. "It is our commitment that you should be able to take something away from this confer-ence that you could utilize in your work situation," Stephen D. Powell, MPI's new president, told me. In the near future, he hopes, the association's educational function will become more formal as MPI inaugurates a meeting-planner certifica-tion program. Planners who qualify will stop being known as planners and start being known as Certified Meeting Profes-sionals.

The teaching at the conference began right after break-fast with a keynote address by John D. "Jack" Jackson, an American Airlines flight instructor who had given such an interesting speech at a previous MPI convention that he had been asked to give it again at this one.

"Most times most change is born of adversity," Jackson said, striding back and forth across the stage, his voice the voice of an evangelist. The theme of his speech, and of the convention, was "Catch the Spirit." He talked about how worried meeting planners were about being laid off or fired or forced to work only part-time. He said that planning was becoming a woman's business, and, indeed, most of the people listening seemed to be women. "You burn out quick in here," he said. "That's why you're so young." He talked about "phenomenons." He talked about "corporate Kitty Litter problems" (that's where everything looks okay on the surface, "but don't dig around"). He spent the first half of his speech telling us not to be afraid of change, to keep up with change, to use change to our advantage. Then he spent much of the rest of his speech making fun of fast food, teenagers, rock music, transistors, Polaroid photographs—in short, making fun of change.

After Jackson, who got a standing ovation, came an audiovisual presentation about *Megatrends*, John Naisbitt's bestselling book about "the America we are becoming," according to the voice that introduced it. "Swedes will become more Swedish," the *Megatrends* presentation predicted. Slides of Swedes flashed onto the screen. They looked, indeed, very Swedish—more Swedish than I had remembered. "The days of the simple either/or are over," the narrator continued. "It's a Baskin-Robbins society." In other words, there are thirty-one flavors of just about everything nowadays. Model T's came only in black; now there are many colors of car. A good point! The wonderful thing about *Megatrends* is that its lessons can be applied to any situation. Naisbitt flatters his readers by telling them what they already believe and claiming that it's a vision of the future.

After *Megatrends* I went to a seminar called "Site, Location and Negotiation" along with about seventy-five other people. Our instructor warmed us up with a not entirely successful joke about Bo Derek in heaven and then said that "the best negotiation is one in which everyone wins." He told us he was very good at planning meetings and then listed some of the concessions he was accustomed to winning from hotels and airlines in return for giving them his business: "a one-for-thirty-five comp [that is, one complimentary hotel room for every thirty-five rooms he booked] . . . fifteen-dollar gift in all rooms . . . ten-dollar-a-gallon coffee with comp danish . . . comp VIP dinner . . . comp liquor . . . unlimited Supersaver airfare with no restrictions . . . up to twenty walkie-talkies completely complimentary." People occasionally oohed and ahhed. As has been the case in every classroom I've ever sat in, the females generally wrote down everything while the males looked around.

A meeting of meeting planners is really two meetings rolled into one. First, it's a regular meeting. Second, it's an *example* of a regular meeting, a sort of metameeting. At the regular meeting the attendees eat terrible food, listen to boring speeches, and take part in boring seminars. It's just like any other meeting. But at the metameeting the attendees view every meal, speech, and seminar as a failed or successful representation of an abstract ideal of meetingness. When our instructor told us that he always demanded thirty-inch tables in the meeting rooms he booked, we all looked down and discovered with horror that our tables were only eighteen inches deep. The tables were inconvenient in and of themselves, but they were also disappointing *philosophically*.

After the session, which lasted an hour, it was time to eat again. At conventions, as on vacations, almost all you ever seem to do is eat. Lunch was thin slabs of roast beef served on pieces of rye bread. Each piece of bread was almost exactly the same size as each piece of meat. This made the meat look thicker, but it also soaked up all the juice, leaving the meat very dry and the bread very wet. The kitchen ran out of plates after half the people at our table had been served, so we fidgeted for a while. The woman sitting next to me, whose job was planning meetings for Canadian lawyers and bankers, said she never worried about menus. "Lawyers and bankers like to drink," she said. "We always have a bar to take their minds off the food."

Actually, I like convention food. I like it for the same reason I like airplane food: It's made of real food, but it's softer, shinier, and sweeter. Also, everybody gets the same thing and you never know what you're having until it's served, if then: the thrill of the unknown. Convention desserts, however, are terrible. Ours was some sort of whipped product that looked like spackling compound. While we dabbed at it with our spoons, a woman in a big red hat went to the microphone and described San Francisco, where the next MPI convention will be held, as a place where "there is much awaiting for your every interest." She was followed by a slide show that recommended the same city as an ideal convention location "for the meeting planner with dreams to weave." The theme of the San Francisco convention will be "Rhythm of the Bay."

After lunch there were more educational seminars. However, nobody went to them. Most MPI members had decided to go off and weave their dreams somewhere else. The escalator was so jammed with escaping attendees that I wondered for a moment if the building was on fire. I walked past a session called "Mapping Your Meeting" in which a handful of cranky-looking people were watching an instructional film starring the Muppets. I dropped in on a sparsely attended session called "Basic Meeting Tools," but after a few minutes—"Hotel service is so bad it staggers your imagination," the instructor was saying—my eyelids got very heavy and I went up to my room to take a nap.

Just as I was drifting off to sleep I had a thought that sent me burrowing through my pile of free stuff for the complimentary notepad I had received in my convention packet. The thought was this: A convention is not a very efficient forum for communicating educational information to a large group of people; why not publish a newsletter instead? I wrote that on my notepad, and then I went to sleep.

*E*xecutives of MPI and other associations spend a lot of time talking about their commitment to learning, but if you look at the advertisements in convention magazines you get an idea of what really appeals to conventioneers. In one ad, for example, the Industry Hills & Sheraton Resort in California calls itself "The only Los Angeles hotel with 650 acres of meeting room." The accompanying photograph shows a man lining up a shot on one of the hotel's two eighteen-hole golf courses.

Golf is extremely big in the convention industry, although it's hard to know how many courses is enough. Two seems to be the most popular number. The Woodlands Inn and Conference Center in Texas has three. Florida's Sandpiper Bay Resort ("Our meeting room is 1000 acres") claims four. Rancho Bernardo Inn in San Diego has two and a half—a shrewd compromise between necessity and extravagance—not to mention a golf "Centre" and a tennis "College." What it really needs is a vocabulary college. "Banquets," says the ad, "will be served with a flare as seen in European hotels."

At hotels, like Stouffer's Riverfront, that have no golf courses, colleges, or flaming meals, there are still plenty of opportunities for entertainment. For example, you can hire Ray Bloch Productions, Inc., a company that offers "Speakers & Lecturers, Music & Entertainment, and Computerized Robotrons." A couple of years ago the Westin Galleria Hotel in Houston threw a full-scale indoor rodeo, complete with greased pigs and bucking broncos, for the American Academy of Pedodontics. They'll throw one for you, too. If you hold your meeting in Britain, you might follow the advice of Donna Zack in a recent issue of *Meetings and Conventions* magazine and arrange a "medieval banquet" featuring "traditional English fare and grog served by bawdy wenches as jesters, minstrels, tumblers and jousters entertain." Jousting at dinner? Okay! Closer to home, Marriott offers "limbo parties" and "shipwreck parties where your group members dress up as the 'pirates.' "

*I*n all this frenzy to cash in on meetings and conventions, one important fact has been overlooked: The convention industry, though large, is not growing. The dollar total has been stuck around $16 billion for several years. "In the past decade," says an article in a recent issue of *Meetings and Conventions*, "there has been a 27 percent increase in the number of cities seeking convention business, but only a 7 percent increase in the amount of business itself." In the words of

Lewis C. Miller, a hotel investment manager at The Pruden-
tial Insurance Company of America, "the lodging industry
must believe that the laws of supply and demand have been
suspended."

One city where the laws of supply and demand have been
rediscovered is Casper, Wyoming. Not long ago, Casper built
a $14 million convention center because, in the words of one
official, "everybody else was building one." Shortly after the
center was completed, the citizens of Casper discovered what
many of the rest of us have known all along, which is that
there aren't all that many people in the world who dream of
attending conventions in Casper, Wyoming. A similar discovery is about to be made by the citizens of Rochester, New
York. Rochester is building a $40 million convention center.
The mayor is excited, despite the fact that in 1982, the year
construction began, the new convention center in Buffalo,
some seventy miles away, was pulling in only half the business
its planners had expected.

Building even an unsuccessful convention center is extremely complicated. According to an article in *Meetings and
Conventions*, it generally requires many years of "planning,
promoting, pleading, promising, politicking, plus putting"—
and here the muse of alliteration nods—"together what can be
a very complicated financial"—ahem—"package."

One such financial package has been put together for a
big new convention center in New York City. The project has
been plagued by design flaws, corruption, and incompetence,
and construction is so far behind schedule that a number of
conventions have already had to cancel. One cancellation came
from the Pittsburgh Conference on Analytical Chemistry and
Applied Spectroscopy, a group that, if it had any civic pride,

would book itself into the new convention center in Pittsburgh, which is already so unpopular that it's never expected
to break even.

Actually, convention centers are almost never expected
to break even. "In a sense they are designed to be loss lead-
ers," Robert Imperata, an official at the Pittsburgh facility,
said not long ago. Cities and states are willing to lose a certain
amount of money on convention centers, because of the ancil-
lary revenues they generate. In 1982 in New York City, for
example, 4.12 million conventioneers spent $821 million. The
money went to hotels, restaurants, prostitutes, car rental
agencies, and all the other businesses that travelers depend
on when they're away from home. It also helped boost tax
collections, thereby feeding money back to the state and local
governments that made all that spending possible in the first
place.

This, at any rate, is how governments justify the expense
of building convention centers. But the figures are deceptive,
because they represent only one side of the convention equa-
tion, the only side convention boosters ever look at. While it
may be true that out-of-town conventioneers spend a great
deal of money in New York, it is also true that New Yorkers
spend a great deal of money at conventions in other cities—
money they might have spent in New York if they'd stayed
at home. If a city exports more conventioneers than it im-
ports, it develops a convention-spending deficit. Easier than
building a convention center, and more immediately profitable, would be to forbid local residents to attend conventions
in other cities.

Although cities and states make money on convention-
generated sales taxes, they lose money on income-tax deduc-

tions. When a New Yorker goes to Pittsburgh for a convention, Pittsburgh, Pennsylvania, and the federal government all earn tax revenues—but New York City, New York State, and the federal government lose revenues, because the attendee writes off what he spends on his trip.

These basic though unacknowledged economic truths point up the grand dilemma of the convention business. Since the industry has been essentially stagnant for years, the only way one city can attract new business is by stealing it from another. When Rochester decided to build its convention center, it did so not because it expected a sudden increase in conventions but because "a consultant's study showed that the lucrative convention business was going to other state's [sic] with new facilities catering specifically to that market," according to a press release from the New York State Urban Development Corporation. In other words, Rochester is building new facilities merely to win back business that was never sufficient to fill its old facilities. The money for the project is coming from the New York State Legislature, which is simultaneously spending ten times as much to help New York City make Rochester's center look second-rate. In the end, Rochester may have to offer its exhibit space, hotel rooms, and restaurant meals at substantial discounts in order to attract any business at all, thereby inflating its already substantial convention deficit. The city will have no choice but to build yet another convention center, enabling it to solve its problem once again by making it even worse.

We had neither pirates nor bawdy wenches at the MPI convention, but we did have Super Sports II. This was a night-time mini-Olympics for MPI members, who were divided into sixteen regional teams. I rode out to the playing field, the site of the 1904 Olympics, on a bus with members of the Canadian squad. Their colors were brown and yellow and their favorite cheer was "Hoser! Hoser!" They didn't have a mascot, although they wanted one. "Something cute," a woman suggested. "Forget about the beaver."

At the Olympic grounds we were greeted by the Steam Heat Dancers, official cheerleaders of the St. Louis Steamers soccer team. Off to the side was a Budweiser beer can the size of a grain elevator. In the distance were tents, potties, an ambulance, two wheelchairs, charcoal grills, and as much beer as I have seen in one place since I graduated from college.

It took nearly an hour for all the teams to assemble. I got a beer and a hamburger and wandered over to a group of men and women wearing togas made from Stouffer's Riverfront Towers sheets. A couple of the men had breadbaskets on their heads. Everyone had a kazoo. A woman who was more nearly out of her sheet than in it experimented with various solutions to this problem. Two people periodically hoisted a banner that said "King Kazoo's Krazies featuring the SLEEZETTES."

When it was time for the games to begin, the Krazies and SLEEZETTES marched around playing that song that is the theme of either the Olympics or ABC Sports. Just before the fast part of the song, they switched to "It's a Small World After All." Then they gathered around a microphone and played "The Star-Spangled Banner." Slowly, people in the crowd began to sing. The music swelled and the entire MPI convention was caught up in a tide of kazooey national pride.

"Southern California, take the field," a voice announced. "Sack race, lane one." The Super Sports looked like so much fun I wished I'd been assigned to a team. In addition to the sack race there was a water-balloon toss, a tug of war, volleyball, an obstacle course, a trivia competition, and an event in which people ran back and fourth putting on parts of baseball uniforms and taking them off again. The Steam Heat Dancers retired to the main tent for Tabs under the watchful eye of a woman who looked like a prison matron. I made frequent trips to the beer wagon and wandered around gazing longingly at the happy attendees. Finally some Canadians asked me to help them fill out their trivia questionnaire. I knew that the mission of the Starship *Enterprise* lasted five years and that the elder Cleavers were June and Ward.

Around nine o'clock, it started to rain. "Balloon toss right after quarter-final tugs," the announcer bellowed. "Remember to hand in your trivia." The public address system crackled as lightning flashed nearby. I stepped away from the metal-tipped tent pole I'd been leaning against and walked out into the rain. A big man with very wet hair offered me a beer he'd been saving for someone else and asked me who I thought would win the tug of war.

When the final balloon had been tossed, we all climbed back on the buses and rode over to the Sheraton-St. Louis for a "Locker Room Wrap-Up." That is to say, a party. We were greeted at the entrance by another marching band and another set of cheerleaders, this time from the Cardinals football team. Sheraton employees in red baseball jackets shook our hands and gave us towels as we walked inside. By the time I had worked my way over to the food, there were two female bodybuilders flexing their muscles in the middle of it. Across the room was a pair of male bodybuilders. Female attendees kept reaching up and stuffing money into the male bodybuilders' swimming trunks. Male attendees, on the whole, were better behaved.

"Now we're gonna take you back," the bandleader said, "to the sound of the Doobie Brothers." The weeks—could it be months?—seemed to slip away. At some point the Cardinal cheerleaders did a big dance routine, which more or less put the female bodybuilders out of business. The Steam Heat Dancers paled in comparison. They were simply in a different league—literally, of course, but also figuratively.

When their dance routine was over, the cheerleaders stayed on the floor and danced with any and all. Then the band played a slow song and the cheerleaders disappeared, poof, just like that. A short while later I ran into several of them by one of the buffets and asked them if they knew who they were cheering for.

"MPI!" they said in unison.

"And what's MPI?"

"Meeting Planners International!"

"And what do they do?"

(Looks of incredulity.) "THEY PLAN MEETINGS!!!!!"

"*R*ecreational activities offer time to network with colleagues," counsels *Working Woman* magazine in an article on conventions. (The article also recommends "networking at breakfast.") But I saw no evidence of networking or even of mentoring at Super Sports II. Everybody was more concerned with drinking beer and winning the balloon toss. And that, I think, is as it should be. A convention isn't a very good place to learn about your business, even if your business is planning conventions. But it's a pretty good place to jump around in a great big sack.

"The meeting planner never gets a damn chance to laugh," Tom Sullivan, the blind golfer from *Good Morning America*, said on opening day. But of course he was mistaken. All the meeting planners I talked to said they'd had a pretty good time at the MPI convention, and especially at Super Sports II. They were less certain, though, about whether it had all been worth the time and expense.

Two men I spoke to said they probably wouldn't bother to come next year unless their companies had surpluses in their travel budgets. On the other hand, a woman told me she had learned enough from a single seminar, "Food & Beverage/ Partners for Profit," to justify the cost of her trip. Maybe she was right, although if a university education cost as much, hour for hour, as a convention education does, nobody in his right mind would send his kids to college.

Will conventions become more conventiony in the America we are becoming? Only John Naisbitt knows for sure. But there's no doubt that conventions will be with us for a very long time. There's even evidence that the industry is on the rebound. The Association of Visitor and Convention Bureaus is predicting a modest increase in convention business for this year, and there are other signs as well. The Southern Baptists, who for years have held their annual conference in church facilities, have finally decided to move into the big time. In 1989 they'll be holding their convention in Las Vegas.

(1983)

My wife recently told me she intends to donate her body to science. I found the proposition ghoulish, even though it would relieve me (I intend to survive her) of the expense of disposal. I said that I was determined to have a more traditional send-off: a waterproof, silk-lined, air-conditioned casket priced in the sports-car range, several acres of freshly cut flowers, a procession of aggrieved schoolchildren winding slowly through some public square, a tape-recorded compilation of my final reflections, and, local ordinances permitting, an eternal flame. But after a bit of research, I have come around to her point of view.

Two powerful human emotions—the fear of death and the love of bargains—inexorably conflict in any serious consideration of what to do with an expired loved one, all the more so if the loved one is oneself. Most people secretly believe that thinking about death is the single surest method of shortening life expectancy.

On the other hand, the appeal of the bargain intensifies

when a third (though essentially unheard-of) emotion—the desire to do good for its own sake—is injected into the discussion. If, after one is entirely finished with it, one's body can be put to some humane or scientific use, enabling life to be preserved or knowledge to be advanced, can one in good conscience refuse? And yet, the mortal coil recoils.

"*N*o freezing in the winter. No scorching in the summer." Such are the advantages of booking space in an above-ground burial condominium, according to a flyer I received not long ago. Printed across the bottom of the page was the following italicized disclaimer: *"We sincerely regret if this letter should reach any home where there is illness or sorrow, as this certainly was not intended."* In other words, if this information has arrived at one of the rare moments in your life when it would actually be of immediate use, please ignore it.

That the funeral business is filled with smoothies, crooks, and con men has been well known since at least 1963, when Jessica Mitford published her classic exposé, *The American Way of Death.* Mitford's book, required reading for all mortals, is filled with fascinating information. Fit-A-Fut and Ko-Zee, she revealed, were the trade names of two styles of "burial footwear," the latter model described by its manufacturer as having "soft, cushioned soles and warm, luxurious slipper comfort, but true shoe smartness." The same company also sold special postmortem "pantees" and "vestees," enabling funeral directors to gouge a few extra dollars out of any family that could be dissuaded from burying a loved one in her own underwear.

Twenty years later, the death industry is unchanged in almost every particular except cost. Mitford found that the average funeral bill, according to industry figures, was $708. When I visited a local mortuary to price a simple burial for a fictitious ailing aunt, the director rattled off a list of probable charges that added up to many times that, flowers and cemetery plot extra. His estimate included $110 for hauling her body two blocks to his establishment and $80 for carrying it back out to the curb. Pallbearing is a union job in New York City; family members can't lay a hand on a coffin without getting a waiver from the Teamsters. ("If they drop the casket, pal, you're gonna be in trouble," a spokesman for Jimmy Hoffa's old union told me.) Hairdresser, $35. Allowing "Auntie" (as he once referred to her) to repose in his "chapel" for one day—something he told me was mandatory, despite the fact that I said I didn't want a memorial service and that no relatives would be dropping by—would be $400.

The largest single charge we discussed was for the casket. He used the word "minimum" as an adjective to describe virtually any model in which I expressed an interest that cost less than $1,500. The single wooden coffin in his showroom was "very" minimum ($1,100). The whole genius of the funeral business is in making you believe you're buying a refrigerator or a sofa or even a car instead of a box that will be lowered into the ground and covered with dirt. Since there are no *real* criteria, other than price, for preferring one such box to another, you end up doing things like sticking your hands inside a few models and choosing the one with the firmest bedsprings. "Women seem to like the color coordination," my Charon said in reference to a twenty-gauge steel model (I think it was called the Brittany) with a baby-blue interior.

Since the women he was talking about are dead, that word "seem" is positively eerie.

Cremation is becoming a fairly popular choice among people who think of themselves as smart shoppers. The funeral industry has responded to this trend by subtly discouraging its customers from considering cremation and by making sure that cremation is very nearly as expensive as burial in a box. A pamphlet called "Considerations Concerning Cremation," published by the National Funeral Directors Association, Inc., and distributed by morticians, pretends to be evenhanded but is actually intended to horrify its readers. "Operating at an extremely high temperature [a cremation oven] reduces the body to a few pounds of bone fragments and ashes in less than two hours. . . . Most of the cremated remains are then placed in an urn or canister and carefully identified." This last sentence is the funeral director's equivalent of "Most newborn babies are then sent home with their proper mothers." Earth burial, in contrast, "is a gradual process of reduction to basic elements."

If the funeral business dislikes cremation, it positively abhors the donation of bodies to medical schools, because in such cases the opportunities for profiteering are dramatically reduced—though not, to be sure, eliminated. There is virtually nothing you can do, short of being disintegrated by Martians in the middle of the ocean, to keep a funeral director from claiming a piece of the action when you die. Once again, a pamphlet tells the story: ". . . essential to avoid the possibility of disappointment . . . more bodies available than the maximum required . . . rejection *is* permitted by state law . . . you can expect your funeral director to be of assistance. . . ."

One almost wishes one could die tomorrow, the sooner to savor the pleasure of taking one's business somewhere else.

*E*rnest W. April, associate professor of anatomy at Columbia University's College of Physicians and Surgeons, is the man in charge of Columbia's supply of cadavers. Dr. April shares his office with Rufus, a huge red dog who wandered into his yard one day and doesn't like to be left alone. Also in Dr. April's office are some skulls, an old-fashioned radio, a human skeleton, a spine, a paperback book with a picture of a skull on it, some more skulls, a few microscopes, some big bones on a shelf, and a small plastic bone on the floor (for Rufus).

"Most medical students look forward to receiving their cadaver," Dr. April told me. "Once they have their cadaver they are, from their point of view, in medical school. It's something tangible. There's anticipation, trepidation. In the first laboratory exercise, the students basically come up and meet the cadaver, almost as if it were a patient."

As at all medical schools, Columbia's cadavers are donated. Prospective benefactors eighteen years of age and older fill out anatomical bequeathal forms and return them to the university. Hours, days, weeks, months, or years pass. "When the Time Comes," as one brochure puts it, the donor's survivors call the medical school's department of anatomy. "Within the greater metropolitan area," the brochure says, "arrangements for removal of the body can be made by the medical college. Alternatively, the family may engage a local funeral director to deliver the **un**embalmed body to the medical college at the address on the cover." Medical schools almost always require unembalmed bodies because ordinary cosmetic embalming, the kind sold at funeral homes, turns skin to the consistency of old shoes and doesn't hold off deterioration for more than a few days. Medical-school embalming, on the other hand, is designed for the ages. "We've had some specimens that we've kept for over twenty years," one professor told me. "It's almost like the Egyptians."

Donated cadavers are stored in a refrigerated room until they're needed. Columbia has a class size of about 200. The ideal student-to-cadaver ratio is four to one (which means "every two people get one of everything there's two of," a medical student explains). Contrary to what the funeral directors say, Columbia, like many schools, has fewer bodies than it would like and so must assign five students to each. Ratios as high as eight to one are not unheard of. If the donor consents beforehand, a cadaver bequeathed to one institution may be transferred to another with greater need. New Jersey, for some reason, attracts almost as many cadavers as it does medical students and occasionally ships extras to New York. (That's extra cadavers, not extra medical students.) People who don't like the idea of being dissected by students at all can specify on their bequeathal forms that their bodies are to be used only for research. Surgeons sometimes practice new or difficult operations on such cadavers before attempting them on living people.

"If a person donates his remains for biomedical education and research," Dr. April says, "there's a moral obligation on our part to utilize the body on this premise if at all possible, and only for that purpose. The only exception is that we occasionally do make material which has been dissected available to art students, because going back to the times of Leonardo da Vinci, Raphael, Titian, and Michelangelo, artists have had a real need to know and understand anatomy." Subscribers to public television, among others, should find this prospect irresistible: a chance to benefit science *and* the arts.

When Columbia's anatomy courses end, the cadavers are individually cremated and buried in a cemetery plot the university owns. All of this is done at the university's expense. (In comparison with funeral home rates, medical school officials estimate that picking up, embalming, storing, cremating, and burying each cadaver costs about $400). If the family so desires, the uncremated remains can be returned to it at the end of the course, as long as the family gives notification beforehand and agrees to cover any extra costs.

*N*early all medical schools operate donation programs much like Columbia's. All you have to do is call up the anatomy department at the nearest medical school and ask what the procedure is. A group called the Associated Medical Schools of New York, based at Manhattan's Bellevue Hospital, oversees donations to a dozen or so institutions around the state, including the New York College of Podiatric Medicine and the New York University School of Dentistry. You might think that a podiatrist and a dentist could share a single cadaver, but no school will take less than a whole body.

I sent away for donation information from dozens of medical schools and state anatomical boards. Studying the resulting avalanche of brochures has given me more than a week of intense reading pleasure, making me feel at times like a young girl poring over brides' magazines in hopes of discovering the perfect honeymoon. Comparison shopping for a place to send one's corpse, like all consumer activities, quickly becomes a joy independent of its actual object. There are many factors to consider.

For example, I knew an elderly man who pledged his body to Harvard. When he died last year, his wife contacted a local funeral home to make arrangements and was told it would cost about a thousand dollars above and beyond the standard fee paid by Harvard. When the widow properly balked (all they had to do was drive the corpse fifty miles) the mortician supplied an eight-page letter justifying his charge. "The possibility that a body may be rejected by the Medical School," he wrote, "would make us less than totally honest if we didn't make you fully aware of same." This sentence conjures up unwanted images of admissions committees, and obliquely suggests that if my friend had aimed a little lower in the first place, the problem might never have arisen.

Medical schools do reserve the right not to honor pledges. All schools turn down bodies that have been severely burned, for obvious reasons. Other requirements vary. Pennsylvania rejects bodies that are "recently operated on, autopsied, decomposed, obese, emaciated, amputated, infectious, mutilated or otherwise unfit." Contagious diseases are particularly worrisome; anatomists keep a careful watch for Jakob-Creutzfeldt disease, a slow-acting virus that kills not only the occasional medical student but also cannibals who dine on the brains of their victims. All schools, as far as I can tell, accept bodies from which the eyes and thin strips of skin have been removed for transplantation; removal of major organs, however, is almost always unacceptable, which means that organ donors (see below) generally can't also be cadaver donors. Pennsylvania is more lenient in this regard. Most other schools want their cadavers intact, although the University of Kansas will accept bodies from which no more than "one extremity has been amputated." (Kansas also asks donors to fill out a form that asks for, among other things, "present" height and "present" weight.)

Stanford's brochure is full of high sentence and King Jamesian resonances, the sort of prose selective colleges use to dishearten hoi polloi. One section lists five grounds for rejection, each beginning with the phrase, "The Division of Human Anatomy will not accept . . ." One thing the Division of Human Anatomy will not stand for is "the body of a person who died during major surgery," which sounds like the medical equivalent of refusing to cross a picket line. The section concludes, *"In summary, the Division of Human Anatomy reserves the right to refuse any body which is, in the opinion of the Division, unfit for its use."*

Most brochures also deal with final disposition of remains. "Ashes can be sent by Parcel Post and interred or scattered in some favorite place," says one donation form. "Bear in mind, before scattering ashes, that they consist of soft bone fragments. Before scattering them on land it is wise to make sure they are pulverized. This is not difficult." But there is not one word about how to do it.

"*C*hances are, you have a long and healthy life to live. But a lot of other people don't. . . ." This curiously comforting thought comes from a pamphlet called "The Gift of Life," published by a Cleveland outfit called Organ Recovery, Inc. Since there's usually no way to tell whether your organs or your whole body will be more useful until When the Time

Comes, the wisest course is to promise everything to everyone
and leave it to the experts to sort things out later.

Organ donation has been given a lot of publicity in recent
years. Drivers' licenses in most states now have tiny organ
pledge forms on the back. These forms may not have much
legal meaning. At New York's Presbyterian Hospital, for in-
stance, no one will remove an organ (or cart away a cadaver
to a medical school) unless the next of kin give their consent.
You could die with an organ-donor card in every pocket, and
another one pasted to your forehead, and still no one would
touch you if your current or separated but not divorced
spouse, son or daughter twenty-one years of age or older,
parent, brother or sister twenty-one years of age or older, or
guardian, in that order, said no. Prince Charles carries a donor
card; if he dropped dead (God save the King) at Presbyterian,
someone would have to get permission from Princess Diana
before removing anything. If you want to be an organ donor,
carrying a card is probably less important than making sure
your relatives know your wishes.

No matter how thorough you are about clearing the way,
however, the chances are extremely slim that your heart,
liver, kidneys, or lungs will ever be transplanted into somebody else. Only about one percent of all the people who die
are potential kidney donors, and kidneys are actually removed
from only one in five of these. The reason the numbers are so
small is that a suitable organ donor is that rarest of individuals, a person in marvelous health who is also, somehow, dead.
Major organs for transplantation have to be removed while
the donors' hearts are still beating, which means that all ma-
jor-organ donors are brain-dead hospital patients whose res-
piration is being maintained artificially.

"Many of the individuals that I'm called to see have died or will die as a result of a major intracranial catastrophe," says John M. Kiernan, transplant coordinator at Presbyterian Hospital. "They may be victims of a gunshot wound, whether self-inflicted or as a result of a homicide, a blunt trauma to the head sustained in an automobile accident, or, to give a recent example, I just had a young fellow who had been struck repeatedly on the head with a baseball bat. These are by definition respirator-dependent patients in total, irreversible coma. They have sustained destruction of the contents of the brain to the level of the spinal cord." We've all been moved by tearful appeals from parents whose children are in desperate need of transplantable organs; we seldom stop to think that the "miracle" for which these parents are praying is the sudden death of another child.

Every organ donor must be pronounced utterly and irretrievably deceased by two separate physicians who will not be involved in the ultimate transplantation. They are not goners; they are gone. This requirement is meant to reassure people who fear that signing organ-donor cards is the rough equivalent of putting out Mafia contracts on their own lives. I used to share these fears; now they strike me as silly.

The bookshelves in Kiernan's office hold volumes with titles like *Brain Death: A New Concept or New Criteria?* Nearby are a few test tubes filled with darkish blood. Behind his door is a big blue-and-white picnic cooler that he uses to carry transplantable organs from donors to recipients. Big blue-and-white picnic coolers seem to be the industry standard for moving organs, whether across town or across the country. In a cover story on liver transplants last year, *Life* magazine published a picture of a man hoisting a cooler called a Playmate Plus into the back of a station wagon. The cooler contained a liver packed in ice.

If your major organs don't make it (because, say, you've lived a long time and faded away slowly in your bed), there's still hope for lesser service. Almost anyone can give skin, eyes, and bone, often without hurting one's chances of getting into medical school. Small strips of skin (whose removal does not disfigure a cadaver) are used to make dressings for burn victims. These dressings help keep many people alive who might die without them. Several parts of the eye can be transplanted; there are perhaps thirty thousand people now blind who would be able to see if enough of us followed the example of Henry Fonda and Arthur Godfrey and donated our corneas. Bone transplants eliminate the need for amputation in many cancer cases. The National Temporal Bone Banks Program of the Deafness Research Foundation collects tiny inner-ear bones and uses them in medical research.

None of these programs saves you burial costs the way donating your whole body will. Nor can you receive money for giving all or part of yourself away. Paying for bodies is widely held to be unseemly and is, in fact, against the law. On the other hand, physicians do not refuse payment for performing transplant operations. Maybe the law ought to be rewritten to include a little sweetener for the people who make the operations possible. On still another hand, the last thing Washington needs right now is a lobby for dead people, who only vote in Texas and Chicago as it is.

*M*aking an intelligent consumer choice usually entails trying out the merchandise. In this case a test drive is out of the question. But since I had never so much as clapped eyes on an actual dead person before, I asked Columbia's Ernest April if he would give me a tour of his anatomy classroom. He agreed somewhat reluctantly, then led me down precisely the sort of stairway you would expect to be led down on your way to a room full of bodies. The classroom, by contrast, was cool and airy and had a fine view of the Hudson River. Blue walls, green floor, bright lights, a big blackboard, a lighted panel for displaying X rays, videotape monitors hanging from the ceiling, lots of enormous sinks for washing up.

Also, of course, the bodies. There seemed to be about thirty of them, each one lying on a metal table and covered with a bright yellow plastic sheet. The only noticeable odor in the room was the odor of new plastic, familiar to anyone who has smelled a beach ball. Since the course was drawing to an end, the shapes beneath the sheets were disconcertingly smaller than expected: as dissection progresses, students tag the parts they're finished with and store them elsewhere. To demonstrate, Dr. April pulled back the yellow sheet on the table nearest us, causing a momentary cessation of my heartbeat and revealing the top of a skull, a set of dentures, a long striated purplish thing, some other things, I'm not sure what else. But no arm, the object of his search. Far across the room, a few students were huddled over a dark form that suggested nothing so much as the week after Thanksgiving. My initial queasiness subsided and, with a sort of overcompensating enthusiasm, I asked if I could bound across the hall for a closer look. Dr. April gently persuaded me to stay put. "This is late in the course," he said softly. "It's not particularly pleasant."

Unpleasant, yes; but is it disgusting or unbearable? Many people say they can't stand the thought of being dissected;

much better, they say, to be fussed over by a funeral director and eased into a concrete vault, there to slumber intact until awakened by choirs of angels. But death is death, and every body, whether lying on a dissection table, baking in a crematorium, or "reposing" in a $10,000 casket, undergoes a transformation that doesn't lend itself to happy contemplation. In terms of sheer physical preservation, a medical school cadaver is vastly more enduring than the recipient of even the costliest ministrations of a funeral director. No casket ever prevented anyone from following the road that Robert Graves described in *Goodbye to All That:* "The colour of the faces changed from white to yellow-grey, to red, to purple, to green, to black, to slimy." The transformation takes days, hours.

Morticians sew corpses' lips together, bringing the needle out through a nostril. Lips are pinned to gums. Eyes are covered with plastic patches, then cemented shut. Orifices are plugged. To prevent loved ones from belching, howling, or worse as the accumulating gases of deterioration escape through any and all available exits, funeral home employees press hard on their abdomens immediately before family "viewings." Makeup is slathered on. Abdomens are drained. Leaks are patched. Unsightly lumps and bulges are trimmed away.

The trouble with death is that *all* the alternatives seem so bleak. It isn't really dissection that appalls; it's mortality. It may be gross to be dissected, but it's no less gross to be burned or buried. There just isn't anything you can do to make being dead seem pleasant and appealing. And barring some great medical breakthrough involving interferon or Jane Brody's column in *The New York Times*, every single one of us is going to die. We should all swallow hard and face the facts and do what's best for the people who will follow us.

Which is why you would think that doctors, who spend their entire lives swallowing hard and facing facts, would be the eagerest anatomical donors of all. But they are not. Of all the people I interviewed for this essay—including several heads of anatomical donation programs, a number of medical students, physicians, even the chief medical examiner of New York—only *one* of them, Ernest W. April, had pledged any part of his body to scientific study or transplantation. And April is a Ph.D., not an M.D. "I don't know of any medical student who is going to give his body," a medical student told me.

Do doctors know something? Does it, maybe, *hurt?* Of course not. Every profession lives in secret horror of its methods. Most reporters I know don't like to be interviewed. But society would crumble if we weren't occasionally better than those who believe themselves to be our betters.

Morbid humor at their expense is one thing future cadavers worry about. Medical schools are aware of this and take pains to keep jokes to a minimum. Still, a certain amount of horsing around is inevitable. Michael Meyers, the man who played Ali McGraw's brother in *Goodbye, Columbus* and went on to become a physician, described some dissection highjinks in a book called *Goodbye Columbus, Hello Medicine*. "By the second week of gross anatomy," Meyers wrote, "it was interesting to notice which members of the class really rolled up their sleeves and dug in (no pun intended—although one group of students did nickname their cadaver 'Ernest,' so they could always say that they were 'digging in Ernest') . . . ," and so on and so on. This is a level of comedy that I do not, to be

perfectly frank, find intimidating. And a cadaver donor who
wanted to have the last laugh could arrange to have an ob-
scene or hilarious message ("Socialized Medicine"?) tattooed
across his chest. Beat them to the punchline. I don't recall
reading anywhere that humorous tattoos are grounds for rejection, even at Stanford.

As for dissection itself, it's about what you would expect.
"You work through the text," says a young woman just beginning her residency, "and by Halloween you've gotten to
the hands. Well, we had a girl in our group who wanted to be
a surgeon, and she did the most amazing thing. She dissected
off the skin *in one piece*. It was like a glove. It was beautiful.
And then there was mine. It looked like someone had been
cracking walnuts. Little flecks, you know? The surgeon had
this glove, and I had this whole series of little flecks. And then
this graduate student comes up and says, 'Have you found the
recurrent branch of the medial nerve?' And I start looking
through my pile. . . ."

A first dissection, like a sexual initiation, is likely to be a
botched job: long on theory and good intentions, short on practical know-how. Results improve with practice, but early
impressions linger. No wonder medical students don't like the
idea of being dissected. For many of them, anatomy class is
their first real experience of death. Maybe it's a good thing if
physicians develop, right from the beginning, an overpowering abhorrence of cadavers. We are all better served if our
physicians devote their energies to keeping us from turning
into the things they hated to dissect in medical school. Anatomy classes, in a sense, trick grade-grubbing medical students
into developing something like a reverence for human life.

Donating one's body is an act of courage, but it's not a

martyrdom. Medical students may not comprehend the magnitude of the gift, but so what? I confess I sort of like the idea of one day inhabiting the nightmares of some as yet (I hope) unborn medical student. And if my contribution means that my neighborhood mortician will go to bed hungry, shuffling off to his drafty garret in the Fit-a-Fut coffin shoes I decided not to buy, then so much the better. Dying well is the best revenge.

(1983)

IV.
ECSTASY IN LIVERPOOL

Charles F. Rosenay's surname wasn't getting the job done anymore. So he did what anyone would have done and had three exclamation marks legally appended to it. Rosenay!!! (as his driver's license now identifies him) is twenty-five years old. He lives with his parents in New Haven, Connecticut. He is the editor and publisher of *Good Day Sunshine*, a Beatle fan magazine that appears irregularly and contains, among other things, letters like this one: "Your magazine is much better and overrules all other Beatle news-letters, which come as cheap-copied paper just thrown to-gether. Yours is like a magazine right off the newsstand!" Rosenay!!! also puts on an annual Beatle convention and does a modest trade in Beatle memorabilia.

Rosenay!!!'s exclamation marks are like a private Lennon-McCartney refrain (Yeah! Yeah! Yeah!). He so cherishes the memory of his favorite musicians that he would rather spend four nights in the Liverpool Holiday Inn than, say, an entire week in Buckingham Palace. (A book called *The Beatles'*

England, which Rosenay!!! owns, dismisses the palace as a
tedious old pile that "finally made a name for itself in 1965
when the Beatles were invited by Queen Elizabeth II to become Members of the British Empire, which allowed them
discounts in many of London's theatres.") Not long ago he got
the chance to make the pilgrimage of his dreams. Along with
sixty-six other Americans, he paid $895 and traveled 3,500
miles in order to spend eight days tramping around London
and Liverpool, following in the footsteps of the Beatles.

I went, too. In fact, Rosenay!!! and I were roommates.
The tour we joined was organized by Tony Raine, a British
expatriate who now runs a country inn in Ogunquit, Maine.
Raine wrote a term paper about the Beatles when he was in
high school, back in the early 1970s. Last year he decided
there might be a future in showing American tourists the very
sidewalk where Ringo Starr used to walk. He formed a company called Rock Apple Tours, placed a few discreet ads in
publications like Rosenay!!!'s, and was overwhelmed by the
response.

The group he put together for his first tour represented
a substantial slice of American life. There was a music teacher
and a Mississippi River tugboat crewman, a plumber and a
data processor, a travel agent and a newspaper copy editor,
a hairdresser and a man who sells cement. There were also
half a dozen secretaries, a man who works on Wall Street,
two single parents accompanying teenaged daughters, a man
who makes his living putting wristwatches into packages, two
Filipino girls who won their trips in a contest, and a young
woman who decided to forego a desperately needed new car
in order to come.

Not all of these people loved the Beatles better than

money or oxygen. Some of them signed up simply because they wanted to take an inexpensive trip to England. But more than a few of them—including one woman who had tried to kill herself (twice) when John Lennon was murdered—entertained feelings about the Fab Four that cannot honestly be described as normal.

Most of the group were also new to England. Some had never flown on an airplane before, much less posed for a passport photo. This occasionally produced confusion. Shortly before the tour departed, Tony Raine received an urgent late-night telephone call from someone!!!'s mother. She had been studying her son's itinerary and had failed to consider the difference in time zones.

"Why does it take twelve hours to get there," she demanded, "and only two hours to come back?"

*S*hortly after sunrise on our first full day in England, the members of the Rock Apple Tour sat down to a hearty breakfast in the dining room of our London hotel. While we ate, a dark-eyed tour member with a 1964 Beatle haircut walked slowly through the room recording the event on movie film. Enormous cardboard identification tags dangled from every sector of his person. American tourists are often faulted for not being interested in other people's countries. But the Rock Apple Tourists were microscopically attentive to detail. The previous afternoon, some six hours after our arrival at Heathrow, a young man from New Orleans had told me that he'd just taken his 108th photograph of the trip.

After breakfast we boarded a pair of touring buses and set out for EMI's Abbey Road Studios, where the Beatles did virtually all of their recording. Along the way our guide, the celebrated Beatles scholar Mark Lewisohn, pointed out historical landmarks. "On your right you see the Royal Albert Hall," he said, "made famous in the Beatles song 'A Day in the Life.' " Camera shutters whirred, making a sound like locusts descending on the autumn harvest. The driver steered cautiously down a narrow street. "On the left is George Harrison's business office," Lewisohn noted, adding cruelly, "and there's quite a possibility that he may even be there today." So many bodies flung themselves from starboard to port that the vehicle was momentarily in danger of capsizing. Cameras clicked frantically. We were so close to the building that focusing was out of the question. "Stop! Stop!" people screamed. But the traffic was too heavy. George's office, perhaps even George himself, grew small behind us. A sad, desperate voice cried out: "I want to go *back!*"

The buses moved on inexorably. Lewisohn called our attention to a street "where Brian Epstein had a flat." By now the Beatle pilgrims had whipped themselves into such a lather of devotion that it did not occur to some of them that he was talking about an apartment and not a punctured tire. They aimed their cameras at the ground.

Many thousands of photographs later, we arrived at Abbey Road, a difficult thoroughfare to find since signs identifying it are usually stolen the instant they are put up. The surrounding area is quiet and mostly residential. Trees line the streets. You could live there for years without realizing you were on sacred ground—if it weren't for all those intense-looking Americans wandering around with crowbars.

The Beatles' debut at Abbey Road twenty years ago was not entirely auspicious: having flunked an audition at Decca, they won a modest contract from EMI and spent two agonizing weeks recording their (agonizing) first single, "Love Me Do." The studios are usually closed to the public, but the group's old quarters were being modernized, so EMI decided, for the first time ever, to let people in.

When we actually set foot in the sanctum sanctorum, the music lilting from the public address system was a choir of anonymous violins making symphonic soup of "I Want to Hold Your Hand"—Beatle Muzak, and at Abbey Road of all places. The effect was jarring, all the more so because the very ground was littered with genuine and nearly genuine Beatle artifacts: a left-handed bass with Paul's signature on the back, an old microphone once bathed by the breath of John Lennon, some recording equipment used to make Beatle records, a "simulated" Beatle drum kit. Almost everyone took a whack at the snare drum or a plink at the venerable Steinway. A transported pianist stumbled blissfully through "Let It Be" and "Imagine." Self-consciousness evaporated in the face of so much touchable stuff. Someone put on a set of headphones and pretended to sing into one of the mikes. A young man in the back of the room, momentarily insensate, took a photograph of a photograph.

Then the lights dimmed and we settled down to watch an excellent film called "The Beatles at Abbey Road." Woven into the sound track were several unreleased recordings, including an early song called "Leave My Kitten Alone" and a wrenchingly beautiful acoustic version of "While My Guitar Gently Weeps." There were also many funny moments, including a series of failed attempts at producing the jarring guitar chord that opens the song "A Hard Day's Night."

At intermission we were served cookies and orange drink,

refreshments that made one think less of the Beatles than of kindergarten. We sat at little tables with red-and-white-checked tablecloths on them. Everything was very cheery. When the program ended, tour members crushed around an impromptu souvenir stand and threw pound notes at the startled salesclerks, who behaved as though they had never before encountered American citizens unloading an alien currency.

The British commercial instinct at this point is almost vestigial. When I asked a studio executive whether there was any thought of introducing the Abbey Road show to a wider market, he sniffed, "Our prime business is recording, actually." Part of this was studied snobbery, put on specially for the Yanks. But it's also true that Britons are embarrassed by the ardor of American Beatle fans. You have to admire them for being so reluctant to exploit the Lads, but sometimes you just want to pick them up and shake them. Would it really be too tasteless for EMI to air its Beatle relics more frequently than once every twenty years? You don't have to be a Beatle maniac to get a kick out of seeing footage of an impossibly youthful George Harrison wearing a "Stamp Out the Beatles" sweatshirt.

Outside we made innumerable crossings of the road itself, just like you-know-who on their famous album cover. Furious motorists screeched and swerved as all sixty-seven Rock Apple Tourists strode repeatedly from curb to curb. A handful of skeptics then determined, after careful scrutiny of the cover photo, that the historic traverse had actually been made some dozen feet down the road. Sextants and astrolabes were consulted; an authentic crossing was made.

Then it was on to a house once owned by Paul. Charles F. Rosenay!!!—who, with nine Beatle T-shirts and only eight days in which to wear them, had spent the early morning hours in the grip of an existential crisis—led a small flanking action over a low wall and occupied soil actually formerly owned by a former Beatle. At the high front gate, boys lifted girls onto their shoulders so they could snap pictures of the house. A small shrub, its branches lush with souvenirs, was quickly defoliated. A couple of doctors from a local hospital good-naturedly hid their faces in their lab coats, pretending that they were the objects of all the attention. When it was time to leave, Rosenay!!!'s marauders reluctantly stormed back over the wall, taking a casualty in the process: a young woman lost her footing and banged her leg on the stone. A rivulet of blood appeared. "I skinned my knee on Paul's wall," she moaned, in ecstasy.

*T*he most remarkable of the Beatles' many remarkable achievements was making themselves seem so familiar. Most people even remotely of their era know John, Paul, George, and Ringo in a way that goes beyond any actual knowledge of biographical detail. They have the fleshed-out heft of well-made characters in fiction. This is no small accomplishment. It isn't every personality that can burrow itself into the consciousness of strangers and dwell there year after year.

For true Beatle fanatics—some of whom have thought about little else for twenty years—the illusion of intimacy has long since ceased to feel anything like an illusion. Charles F. Rosenay!!! wears his hair like Paul McCartney of the "Let It Be" period. Rosenay!!! clearly understands the difference between himself and his idol, and yet you can tell by the way he makes his eyelids droop at the corners that he sometimes per-

mits himself to believe he knows what it is to be Paul Mc-
Cartney.

Being a Beatle fan always involves choosing a favorite.
"I would say that about seventy percent are Paul fans," a
young woman told me on the bus one day. She was a partisan,
of course, and not above inflating her statistics. John retains
great drawing power even from beyond the grave. When I
was in grade school, liking John best was thought to reflect a
certain depth of intellect. George fans have never been nearly
so numerous, although there is a fan club called The Harrison
Alliance. "The Harrison Alliance has not only its fine quality
printing going for it, but also features fabulous exclusive photographs (which is one of the things that [it] is famous for),"
according to a reviewer. The tricky thing about favoring one
Beatle is that you have to push your man without running
down the others. Actually hating one of the Fab Four would
be unthinkable. Fans who find themselves entertaining negative thoughts usually vent them on Pete Best, the original
drummer, or Paul McCartney's wife. Yoko Ono used to be
despised, but since John's murder her stock has risen.

"I wish I wasn't so into them," a temporary secretary
told me. "I wish I wasn't so analytical. For me it isn't enough
to like them. I've got to know why they mean so much to me."
She was a few days shy of her twenty-ninth birthday. Over
the previous decade she had watched her old friends drift
away—to husbands, families, careers. "A lot of my friends
don't understand," she said. But she had stayed true to Paul,
her favorite. Remaining true to a man she's never met can
take a lot out of a girl—like going into a convent. Still, she
said, "I'm pleased for Paul. I think he's handled his life well,
considering."

Considering? Considering that he's never dropped by to say hello? "He's usually accessible," she said with a certain resignation. "That's what they say. Although I haven't seen him yet." The night before, she and another woman on the tour had stayed up till dawn discussing what the Beatles meant to them. She described them as "four parts of one being." She said her love for them had grown and become sublime as she had, well, matured. "I'm experiencing things that they experienced." The songs affected her more profoundly now than they had when she was young, because now she understood them.

I asked her what she would say to Paul McCartney if she ever had the good luck to meet him. She had several possible scripts, arrived at after many years of careful consideration. "What the heck can I say to you," one of them began, "that hasn't been said a thousand times before?" Not that, probably. Another possibility: "Excuse me, I'm waiting for Paul McCartney. Do you know where he is?" Humor is known to appeal to him. Screaming and fainting are no longer advised. "Just act natural," she counseled, "although ten years ago I wouldn't have agreed."

Of course, each and every one of the (undoubtedly) millions of women around the world who dream of meeting Paul McCartney is convinced that *she* would be more natural, more offhand, more irresistibly authentic than any of the others — if the opportunity to prove it would only arise. Let's see: Paul steps into the elevator one day, you casually deliver the line you've been polishing for the last couple of decades, and before you can say another word he's forgotten about dumpy old Linda Eastman and gotten off at your floor instead of his.

It's like praying, really, all this imaginary chatting with

the Beatles. "I've always used it as a crutch when things are really bad." Times may be tough, but Paul is out there somewhere just being Paul and caring, although in a necessarily general sort of way, about what happens to you.

"It's frustrating that I get this close. I'd just like the chance to find out myself what I would say."

*C*harles F. Rosenay!!! strolled across a parking lot in Stratford-on-Avon eating a Popsicle, carrying a shoulder bag, and wearing high-top basketball shoes, white knee socks, shorts, a Beatle wristwatch, a blue Paul McCartney T-Shirt, and a bobby's helmet. In the background was an advertisement for soft ice cream, a pub called (apparently) GOOD PUB FOOD, an elaborate souvenir stand, throngs of international vacationers. Stratford is a nice place, although in tourist season it tends a little in the direction of Disneyland. Surrounded by camera-toting travelers, its authentically ancient architecture looks bizarrely like a hokey reproduction.

We had stopped in Stratford for lunch on our way to Liverpool. There was some confusion in the ranks as to why a Beatle-free location had been selected for this honor. William Shakespeare was mentioned, producing nods of recognition. On our way out of town, we pulled in at Anne Hathaway's cottage for a quick look. A debate developed as to whether Hathaway had been Shakespeare's mother or his mistress, two erring guesses that neatly bracketed her true identity (she was his wife). "Killed another roll of film," a tour member told me when he climbed back on the bus. For the remainder of the tour, Stratford lingered vaguely in the group's collective memory as Stafford, Stanford, or Stratton.

As the afternoon wore on, the Rock Apple Tour hit spiritual low tide. The day was hot, the highway was crowded, the Coca-Cola at the rest stop was warm. The bus ride dragged on for hours. At one point we were stalled for many minutes in an area where the principal crop seemed to be cow manure. "I wouldn't live in London for anything," a woman said, the drive having soured her on the entire country. "It's too dirty and there's no ice." Some grumbled about the delay in Stratford, others about the lack of air-conditioning. One tour member, perspiration streaming down his face, tried to explain the superiority of American weather to an uncomprehending British photographer: "You see, down in New Orleans, the humidity is so hot . . ." Elsewhere on the bus, a brooding young man muttered to himself under cover of the tape player, pausing now and then to lick his fingers and moisten the end of his nose. When "I Want to Hold Your Hand" came on, he sang along, substituting "ass" for "hand."

Then, magic: Liverpool. The city's smokestacks loomed like the spires of Oz. The sulfuric haze above the skyline parted like a curtain. We had arrived at the birthplace of the Beatles. The day's ordeal was forgotten and the bus came alive.

"There is the 'shelter in the middle of the roundabout,' " our excellent guide, a pretty young woman named Vivienne Greenwood, said as we drove past Penny Lane.

"Where? Where? Where?"

We passed a park bench with three girls sitting on it. "There's some *birds* hanging out!" a boy behind me cried. By now half a dozen tour members had begun to sound suspiciously like Beatles. When the tape player on one of the buses had faltered earlier in the day, a thirtyish man with curly hair had hollered, "What happened to the bleedin' myoosic?"

Vivienne explained that Liverpool was a city with serious problems. She pointed out a block of rundown houses and the shell of a bank destroyed in race riots. But the Rock Apple Tourists were not easily depressed.

"Hey, row houses!"

"I expected worse."

"An American restaurant!"

"It's better than New York."

"It's still pretty clean."

"This is Rodney Street," Vivienne said. "It's known for its many doctors and surgeries. Blackstone was born in Rodney Street."

"Born in the street? No wonder they need doctors."

"Burger Bar!"

"A space needle or something."

"I expected it to be a lot worse."

Cheers erupted when we stopped in front of an honest-to-god Holiday Inn and the driver turned off the engine. The day had been long and hot, but now everything seemed worthwhile.

"Take a look at the rooms," said a voice from up in front. We all looked up. "See those little louvers under the windows? That means *air-conditioning.*"

*T*he big attraction in Liverpool was the Mersey Beatle Extravaganza, a three-day convention and souvenir sale held in a quietly shabby hotel near the center of town. In the main selling area Beatle underpants were going for a pound a pair. A "certified copy" of John's birth certificate was 60 pence, marked down from 75. Color snapshots of various Beatles, mostly Paul, were available for about a dollar each. Also Beatle bookmarks, Beatle pocket mirrors, Beatle scissors, Beatle combs, Beatle nail files (Beatle hygiene is apparently big in Britain), Beatle patches, Beatle key rings, Beatle pens. For ampler budgets there were records, T-shirts, books, magazines, coffee mugs, and imitation Beatle jackets (about $35). I bought some postcards and a little pin. And a skinny black tie that says "The Beatles" on it and that I now realize I will probably never wear.

All in all, I thought, the prices were reasonable—surprisingly so. I've never been to a Beatle convention in the United States, but I'm told the atmosphere is very different. Herds of high-rolling teenagers surge from booth to booth buying forged autographs with hundred-dollar bills stolen from their parents, etc. An American dealer named Scott showed me a poster that he said usually sold for about $10 in the United States; the price in Liverpool was 30 pence, less than half a dollar. Even at these prices, though, British attendees seemed content to leave most of the buying to Americans. (The Rock Apple Tour's aggregate luggage volume approximately doubled during the course of the Extravaganza.) The English, meanwhile, watched movies and drank beer, pints of which were bafflingly less expensive in the auditorium than in local pubs. Attendance, I was told, was down significantly from the year before.

Later in the afternoon I went to a question-and-answer session with Alistair Taylor, who was at one time the Beatles' "office manager and chief fixer." Why did the Beatles get rid of Pete Best? "I just felt that the drum sound wasn't right." Did Brian Epstein know what he was doing? "Brian turned down an Ed Sullivan show, because we didn't have the right

number." ("No!" gasped the moderator.) Would the Beatles
have stayed together longer if Brian Epstein hadn't died?
"The Beatles started breaking up about the second year we
were happening." Funny, I don't remember a Beatle named
Alistair. I must be getting old.

One of the most popular convention speakers was an
American teacher of remedial reading named Joel Glazier.
"Joel also lectures on a course on 'The Beatles' at Delaware
University," said the convention program, "—we wish they
had some courses like that in Britain, imagine majoring in 'The
Beatles'!!!!!" (Rosenay!!! swears he didn't write this.) "My
lecture was on 'Paul Is Dead,' " Prof. Glazier told me after I
had wandered in too late to hear any of it. "I'm trying to write
a book, but no one wants it. They all want Lennon books."
Just his luck to have a Beatle *actually* die—there goes the
market. Glazier was wearing a shirt that said, "TURN ME ON
DEAD MAN," backward. Who made the shirt? "My mother."

After his speech, Glazier peddled three-dollar Xerox
copies of a five-year-old article on his favorite subject
("Whether it was to draw attention to himself by resembling
a corpse is conjecture . . . but [Paul's] explanation of being
barefoot all day does not hold up"). When demand slackened,
he retired to his booth and solicited donations for the John
Lennon Peace Forest, which is in Israel. "John is the most
famous Beatle in Israel," an Israeli Beatle collector told me
later. Did I have any idea how many Beatle collectors there
were in all of Israel? No. "Five."

On the last day of the convention, Victor Spinetti, a man
who played characters in several Beatles movies, was brought
in to "personally authenticate" a truckload of bricks from the
old Cavern Club, where the Beatles started out. The bricks

cost five pounds each. The Cavern Club had been torn down several years before to make way for a parking lot; an exclusive condominium was now being built on the site, which wasn't far from our hotel. "I hope you'll come forward and buy the bricks," Spinetti said. Many people did. One tour member bought five. A long line snaked around the room. Spinetti was suddenly overcome with emotion. "Strawberry Fields forever!" he cried. "Buy the bricks, luvs!"

*O*verall, the Mersey Beatle Extravaganza was pleasantly uneventful. The only dramatic moment came during Joel Glazier's lecture, when an agitated, middle-aged Liverpudlian loudly demanded to know what the Beatles had ever done for his city and then made such a scene he had to be physically removed. Liverpool has wounds no Beatle will ever heal, but the protester had chosen the wrong crowd on which to vent his rage. Beatle fans are probably the only people left in the world who have any genuine faith in Liverpool's future as a place to live. "It's an industrial city but not an industrious one," I had been told by an Englishman who found the idea of spending a holiday there hilarious.

To the Rock Apple Tourists, though, Merseyside looked like the Kingdom of God. In moments stolen from the extravaganza, they paid penitent visits to Strawberry Field, the Cavern Club construction site, Aunt Mimi's old house, Penny Lane (where one girl cried real tears when her camera ran out of film), countless pubs, a memorabilia-filled restaurant called McCartney's Bistro, and many other shrines. People who had ordered tequila sunrises and shifted nervously from foot to foot in London pubs now happily downed pints of bitter and traded slang words and obscenities (the only truly universal language) with local barflies. The noisy conventioneer excepted, Liverpudlians seemed touched—if a little confused—by all the attention: They don't get many tourists up that way.

One tour member, a plumber, made so many friends in Liverpool that he abandoned the tour group altogether in the evenings. The tugboat crewman pitched in backstage at the convention. A girl who had struck me earlier as being terminally shy walked right up to a stranger in a pub and started a conversation. Beatle fanatics who didn't have many friends at home suddenly found themselves surrounded by people with whom they actually shared an interest. On the third night in Liverpool, several tour members tentatively paired off and disappeared; the next morning there were a few surviving couples eating breakfast together.

The biggest Liverpool fan on the tour was Celeste Simone Sabatini. Celeste was born in 1957. She lives in Moline and works as a secretary in her mother's private nursing business. Her father left home when she was two, returned briefly when she was twenty-two, then disappeared. "So it was kind of like what John had," she said, almost proud. She's been a Beatle fan since she was six—a babysitter gave her the group's first album. Her favorite Beatle is John, although over the years she has loved them all. "The guy I went out with said it was an obsession and I ought to get rid of it," she confided. The boyfriend knew something about obsession; he was a self-styled John Lennon look-alike who played guitar in a band called The Beatles Forever.

Celeste bought more than enough Beatle stuff to cover both double beds in her hotel room. She bought a brick and got it signed by the surviving members of the Quarrymen,

John's old group. "They were sitting there and treating me just like everybody else, and they were telling me about John and what he used to do. I thought, Why are they standing here telling *me* this?" In Penny Lane one day she ran into Charlie Lennon, a distant uncle of John's, and talked to him about "fishing and the war." On the telephone later she told her mother she felt like a celebrity.

Never again, for Celeste Sabatini, will America seem like home. She may spend the rest of her life in Moline, but her heart will always be in Liverpool. "When we were in Penny Lane," she said at the end of the trip, "I started to get a tear in my eye, because I don't want to leave."

But of course, the Rock Apple Tourists eventually did have to leave. For one thing, Charles F. Rosenay!!! was beginning to get hungry. During his week in England he subsisted almost entirely on Rice Krispies, chocolate-covered raisins, cookies, and 7-Up. Even so, like virtually everyone else on the trip, he had the time of his life. When he got back to the United States it took him a full week to get used to living on the earth again. Then he sat down and invited all his new friends to a big reunion at his next Beatles convention. Tony Raine, the tour director, offered to provide a bus.

Raine also went to work on Rock Apple Tour II. Abbey Road will be closed to the public again by the time the new group arrives, but Raine isn't greatly concerned. If Britain still isn't ready to worship the Beatles properly, he'll take his pilgrims elsewhere. The Fab Four were Fab all over the world, and Jerusalem is where you find it. The first stop on the new tour, Raine says, will probably be Austria. That's where you have to go if you want to take lessons from the *actual person* who taught the Beatles how to ski.

(1983)

V.
SATELLITE TELEVISION

"**S**page is upon us—The Age of Space," wrote David O. Woodbury in 1957. Making up words and getting people to use them is harder than many people believe. For every *Koreagate* or *maxiskirt* that dances on the tongues of Americans, there are dozens if not millions of neologisms that no one ever uses.

A disproportionate number of these unused words were coined by Woodbury. *Polycom. Astrogation. Rockoon. Plorb.* He used them in a book about the coming age of satellites. "Plorb is short for '*Pl*acing artificial moons in *orb*its,' " he explained. "An inelegant word, perhaps, with a certain similarity to 'Plop!,' which many pessimistic people fear is exactly what the satellite is going to do." Just before the book went to press, the Soviets launched the earth's first plorb and Woodbury discovered with bitter indignation that his entire manuscript was in the wrong tense. Describing himself as "a victim of Russian propaganda," he hastily composed a new preface in which he referred to *Sputnik* as "little," "fat," and "this unwelcome surprise" and suggested that the pioneering Soviet space vehicle be renamed *Propnik*, as it has not been called ever since.

A few chapters later Woodbury fixed his gaze on the future. Thirty years might pass, he speculated, before it would be possible to crash a small satellite into the moon "and perhaps send back a flash of light." Nonetheless, he believed that space travel was just around the corner. "People who are teenagers now will no doubt live to take space weekends, say at some Martian beach," he declared. As to more workaday uses to which space might be put, Woodbury was skeptical. He noted that a few ambitious visionaries had suggested using satellites to transmit television signals, but he doubted that this would come to pass. He wrote, "It is difficult to see how television, as we know it at present, could justify such unrelenting saturation as this might bring about, or the cost."

Today scientists understand that Woodbury was completely wrong about everything. They are quite certain not only that the teenagers of 1957 will never vacation on Martian beaches but also that there *are* no Martian beaches. The true practical value of space has turned out to include precisely the sort of telecommunication that Woodbury believed to be more outlandish than holiday jaunts around the solar system.

The transmission of television and other signals by satellite has become a technological commonplace. Communications satellites now ring the globe. They have made possible improved navigation and flight control, worldwide high-speed data transmission, business teleconferencing, and increased telephone service. (The annoying little delay in most international and many domestic phone calls is the time it takes a microwave, traveling at the speed of light, to zip back and forth between Earth and a satellite.) They have also brought about the rapid expansion of cable television, the wild proliferation of new programming, and in the past few years the birth of a brand new industry aimed at enabling people to receive satellite signals directly in their homes. More than a million Americans now own satellite antennas of varying shapes and sizes. They use them to receive as many as 100 different television channels bearing everything from X-rated movies to unedited network news stories to Russian weather reports to talk shows whose hosts are nuns.

Ten years ago no regular American television programming was transmitted by satellite. Today almost every viewer, whether or not he owns a satellite antenna, watches shows that have spent at least part of their lives bouncing through outer space. The significance of this change is not obvious to most people. Few of us care very much how *Dynasty* gets to our living rooms so long as it gets there intact and on time. Nonetheless, the satellite television revolution, just now getting underway, has the potential to transform the world. It may one day come to be viewed as a more portentous development than the invention of television itself.

Vastly more prescient than David O. Woodbury was Arthur C. Clarke, the famous science-fiction writer. Whereas most science-fiction writers spend their time predicting, say, the discovery of planets ruled by angry, invisible dogs, Clarke has largely confined himself to predicting things that actually come to pass. In 1945, for example—writing in an obscure British publication called *Wireless World*—he laid out the blueprint for the modern system of transmitting television signals by satellite.

Clarke's proposal was prompted in part by the inability of television signals to pass through the ground or bend around the earth. Television stations perch their transmitting antennas on towers, mountains, and skyscrapers in order to increase their broadcast area, but even with such a boost their range seldom exceeds fifty miles. One way to overcome this limitation, Clarke wrote, would be to place TV antennas in space. A satellite circling the earth a hundred miles above the ground—the lowest feasible orbit—would have an enormous broadcast range.

At this altitude, however, a satellite would take only ninety minutes to circle the globe, and that would greatly limit its usefulness as a transmitting station. Television shows would fade in and out as the satellite zoomed past, and viewers would have to adjust their receiving antennas constantly in order to keep them trained on the drifting signal. Clarke pointed out that at a much higher altitude—22,300 miles—a satellite's orbital period would be twenty-four hours, the same time that it takes the earth to turn on its axis. A satellite orbiting at this height directly above the equator would seem to hang motionless in the sky. Its signal could be received with a fixed antenna.

Satellites in this 22,300-mile orbit (now called the Clarke Belt) are often referred to as geosynchronous or geostationary. Clarke suggested launching three of them, such that they would be evenly spaced above the equator. By using them to relay signals between stations on the ground, he wrote, it would be possible to send information almost instantaneously from almost anywhere to almost anywhere else.

The first communications satellites, launched more than a decade later, were anything but geosynchronous. *Echo*, built by Bell Telephone Laboratories and launched by the National

Aeronautics and Space Administration (NASA) into a low orbit in 1960, was just a big metallic balloon that served as a
mirror off which radio signals could be bounced. *Telstar*,
launched in 1962, had an active transponder (or transmitter/
responder, the device that receives a signal, amplifies it, and
passes it along), but it too followed a low orbit that made it
useless for its primary purpose much of the time. Still, *Telstar*
carried the first intercontinental television broadcast—a shot
of an American flag waving over the AT&T earth station in
Andover, Maine. The broadcast was only a test, but it was
intercepted in England and France. The first functioning geosynchronous satellite, *Syncom II*, was launched the following
year. President Kennedy christened it by placing a telephone
call to Abubakar Balewa, the prime minister of Nigeria.

In 1964 American television viewers watched part of the
Tokyo Olympics courtesy of *Syncom III*. Other special events
were broadcast from time to time. But television was not a
priority of early communications satellites, which had to shut
down all their other transmissions (usually telephone calls) in
order to carry a single channel of television. For that matter,
communications satellites were not a priority of the early
space program. America's first genuine domestic communications satellite, *Westar 1*, built by Western Union, wasn't
launched until 1974.

In the fall of 1975 Home Box Office, a fledgling pay-tele-
vision company that had been founded three years earlier by
Time Inc., began using *Westar* to distribute programming to
its cable affiliates. The first offering was the "Thrilla in Ma-
nila," the heavyweight-title fight between Muhammad Ali and
Joe Frazier on September 30. The fight was transmitted live
from the Philippines to HBO cable affiliates serving 15,000
subscribers in Florida and Mississippi.

HBO's decision to transmit regular programming by satellite was viewed at the time as mildly insane. What if the thing fell out of the sky? The networks generally used AT&T's terrestrial microwave links to transmit their shows to stations around the country. Some suppliers distributed programming physically, on videotape. The phone company and the post office seemed comfortingly dependable in comparison with the great beyond. Another factor was cost. In order for an affiliate to receive television signals from a satellite, it needed an earth station—a large dish-shaped antenna, amplifiers, receivers, and other paraphernalia. In 1975 an earth station cost as much as $125,000. This was a formidable investment for a cable operator, who couldn't be certain that anybody else would follow HBO's lead or that HBO would stay in business.

One reason satellite antennas were so expensive in 1975 was that the Federal Communications Commission required them to be enormous—nearly thirty feet in diameter. This requirement was intended to protect cable subscribers from receiving substandard pictures (larger dishes generally produce better signals). But earth station technology improved rapidly, and the FCC relaxed its rules in 1976. By using better receivers and amplifiers, cable operators were able to produce good pictures with dishes less than fifteen feet in diameter. Costs fell dramatically. Today a cable operator using a 4.5-meter dish can set up a commercial-quality earth station for less than $5,000.

As costs fell, HBO entered a period of dizzying growth. More and more cable TV systems bought earth stations and began offering HBO to their customers. The service's subscriber base grew from fewer than 100,000 in early 1975 to more than half a million by the middle of 1976. The drop in prices had another effect, which no one had anticipated: a satellite earth station began to look like something that an ordinary consumer might be willing to buy.

The first American home earth station was built from scratch in 1976 by H. Taylor Howard, a professor of electrical engineering at Stanford. Shortly after HBO began its satellite transmissions, one of Howard's graduate students mentioned to him that transponder 17 on *Satcom 1* (where HBO had moved) was now carrying a television signal. "I simply went home and poured concrete," Howard says. In his garage was an old fifteen-foot microwave antenna that he had acquired one day in the throes of an overpowering urge to own a large, useless thing. He hoisted it into place.

"I literally had to build everything," he says. "I used some surplus components that were available, like the local oscillator and receiver. It was fixed-tuned—only one channel. I used a microwave source that I bought at a surplus store and had to order a crystal for it. That cost a hundred bucks, which was the major cost of the system. It came together very quickly. It's no big deal, actually. It's just a broad-band FM receiver, and there's not a lot to it."

On September 14, 1976, Howard tuned in his first picture. It was HBO, still the only regular American service carried by satellite. About six months later, he wrote to the company explaining that he was picking up its signal on a home-built terminal and offering to pay a monthly fee. He never received a reply.

Over the next few years a growing but still small number of electronics gadgeteers cobbled together their own earth stations. Many of these systems were built according to instructions that Howard published in 1979, in a booklet called the *Howard Terminal Manual*, which its fans refer to as the

Old Testament of the backyard earth-station movement. Howard received some help with his manual from Robert B. Cooper, Jr., the editor of a cable TV trade magazine, who had installed his own dish, a twenty-footer, in Arcadia, Oklahoma, in 1977. Today Howard and Cooper are known as the fathers of satellite television. Cooper publishes *Coop's Satellite Digest*, a fortnightly journal also referred to as the Old Testament of the backyard earth-station movement. Coop has a pipe permanently stuck in his mouth and is a well-known character in satellite circles. He is also a literary stylist with a passion for inverted commas and bold-face type. Reminiscing about the early days of the industry he helped create, he wrote recently,

> My family became the first "Satellite TV Junkie" family in the USA. I would later learn that **Rod Wheeler,** up in the Yukon in Canada, had preceded us with his own terminal by a month or so, and **his family,** living in a log cabin 15 miles from the nearest town, was already "hooked" when we turned on down in Oklahoma. Everything was on horizontal polarization in those days; it would be 1978 before anything came up on vertical and I would be faced with "that" problem.

In 1978, before the full flowering of his prose style, Coop wrote an article for *TV Guide* that is not infrequently referred to as the Old Testament of the backyard earth-station movement. By this time, the major networks had made a few bolder forays into outer space, using satellites to send programming to their affiliates and to receive transmissions from the field. NBC used a satellite to transmit *The Tonight Show* live from Burbank, California, to its headquarters in New York, where

it was edited and taped for later broadcast. "The live version
on satellite is typically sent without 'bleeps' and often without
commercials; during those numerous commercial breaks the
cameras and mikes continue to run 'hot' on the satellite," Coop
explained in *TV Guide*. "Around our house we call this version
'R-rated Carson.' " The networks also used satellites to transmit regional sporting events back to New York, making it
possible for diehard football fans to pick up virtually any NFL
game being played anywhere in the country, even when it was
blacked out in their own city. (Some of the earliest and most
enthusiastic earth-station owners were bookies.)

Several brand-new programming suppliers were also tak-
ing advantage of thitherto unused satellite transponders:
Showtime, a new movie channel that competed with HBO;
WTCG, Ted Turner's Atlanta "super station," now called
WTBS (at about the same time, Turner installed a dish on a
trailer so that on business trips he could watch his station);
and a number of religious channels, including TBN (Trinity
Broadcasting Network), CBN (Christian Broadcasting Network), and PTL (which stands for both People That Love and
Praise the Lord). All these transmissions were intended for
cable-TV operators, who paid fees for the right to include
them in the programming packages that they sold to their
subscribers. But anyone with a dish in his backyard could pick
them up as well.

Space-age television was full of unanticipated pitfalls for
broadcasters. One of the first markets for Turner's super station was a cable system in Hawaii. Turner's station in those
days carried commercials by, among others, local automobile
dealers. When Hawaiian viewers saw how inexpensive used
cars were in Atlanta, they were furious. It did no good to

remind them that they lived in a very nice place where many Georgians would be happy to spend their vacations. Turner's sponsors had to be told to keep their prices to themselves.

Gradually the backyard earth-station movement began to expand beyond its early base of ham radio operators and electronics tinkerers. Farmers, ranchers, and other people who lived in remote areas that would never be wired for cable saw dish antennas as their only chance to get decent reception. Neighbors dropped by to complain about the damned radar station, stuck around to watch a bit of the Canadian broadcast of *Charlie's Angels*, and went home to order dishes of their own. Ten thousand dollars could seem like a reasonable price to pay for dozens of crystal-clear channels where there had been only static before. The number of programs increased, and antenna manufacturers, having exhausted their original market of cable operators, began selling dishes in suburban neighborhoods where reception wasn't a problem: people just wanted to watch a lot of TV. Satellite stores began to pop up in shopping centers. Prices fell further and the equipment became more sophisticated. In the early days earth-station owners had to move their dishes by hand to switch from one satellite to another. Today changing satellites is as easy as changing channels.

The cable business, meanwhile, was continuing to expand, and more and more new programming was turning up on the satellites. The boom led to some interesting juxtapositions. Today on *Satcom F4* the National Christian Network is just five transponders away from the Playboy Channel. In between are Netcom, a network for teleconferencing, Sportsvision (Chicago-area sporting events), American Movie Classics (films at least fifteen years old), and Home Sports

Entertainment (sporting events in Texas, Louisiana, Arkansas, Oklahoma, and New Mexico). On *Westar 5*, forty degrees west of *Satcom F4*, the services include one X-rated network, the Financial News Network, a service that covers regional sports in Michigan, and the University Network, an uncategorizable potpourri masterminded by Dr. Gene Scott, a Stanford-educated evangelist who has been known to raise money for his station by staring into the camera in reproachful silence until his viewers are shamed into contributing. Eleven degrees farther west is *Galaxy 1*, home of, among others, HBO, Showtime, the Cable News Network, the Spanish International Network, the Entertainment and Sports Programming Network, and C-Span, the network that covers Congress. (All this changes from month to month, and even from week to week.)

In the early days picking up satellite broadcasts with backyard terminals was, at best, of dubious legality. Cooper and Turner had licenses from the FCC permitting them to use their antennas for "experimental" purposes. But most other earth-station owners operated in at least apparent violation of the nation's principal broadcasting law, the Communications Act of 1934. In 1934 not even Arthur C. Clarke had anticipated that children in Arcadia, Oklahoma, would one day rush home from kindergarten to watch reruns of *Gilligan's Island* beamed from a point in space 22,300 miles away. When earth-station owners numbered no more than a few dozen, nobody worried very much about the law. But as the number of satellite transmissions increased, and as the number of earth-station owners swelled, programming suppliers, broadcasters, cable operators, and legislators gradually realized that they had a problem on their hands.

In October of 1985 this problem was partly resolved (or at least deferred) by the Cable Communications Policy Act, which made it legal for private citizens to own and use earth stations. But many snags remained. Premium programmers like HBO and Showtime had been annoyed that hundreds of thousands of dish owners were watching their shows for free. The new law made such viewing legal until programmers either scrambled their signals or initiated some sort of marketing scheme that would enable earth-station owners to pay for the television they watched. The premium programmers promised that they would scramble.

While HBO and Showtime fretted about viewers they didn't want, other companies set out to provide programming directly to the backyard market. Calculating that many Americans would be willing to buy satellite systems if the antennas could be made small and cheap enough, a few companies invested hundreds of millions of dollars to build high-powered satellites whose signals would be receivable by dishes just two or three feet in diameter. This still largely hypothetical television service is known as Direct Broadcast Satellite, or DBS. DBS shows signs of being one of the most expensive bad ideas in the history of telecommunications (for reasons that will be explained later), but in the early 1980s it looked to some people like the future itself.

Backyard earth stations, meanwhile, have multiplied far beyond the early imaginings of Taylor Howard and Bob Cooper. Earth-station owners who have time to read can choose from among perhaps a dozen satellite magazines and program guides—including one glossy hundred-page publication devoted solely to the shows on *Galaxy 1*. It is estimated that twenty thousand to forty thousand new stations are being installed every month, and the pace is quickening. A complete home system—including a dish antenna big enough to horrify almost any neighbor—can now be had for less than $2500.

A satellite, it turns out, is surprisingly large. Not long ago I saw several tremendous ones being put together at Hughes Communications, in Los Angeles, a company responsible for many of the "birds" (as they are known in the trade) in the Clarke Belt. The biggest was *Intelstat VI*, an international-communications satellite. When fully deployed in outer space, it will be twelve feet in diameter and nearly forty feet tall—smaller than a grain silo but vastly larger than the stove-sized canister I had been expecting.

Before you can look at the satellites at Hughes, you have to put on a smock—just for "psychological reasons," according to my guide, Emery S. Wilson, Jr. Everyone in the assembly area had one on. Mine was dark blue; Wilson's was light blue. We walked around the immense building and peered into things. Satellites are made of wires, metal strips, aluminum foil, the insides of old televisions, and a number of items too technical to be of interest to the general reader. There was a piece of space shuttle in one corner. Some engineers were working on a satellite for Australia that will bring television not only to the outback but also to Papua New Guinea. Nearby were a couple of huge space-simulation chambers for testing new birds. Space-simulation chambers! But it turns out that weightlessness is one thing the chambers can't simulate.

Hughes's best-selling bird is the HS 376. *Galaxy 1* and *Westar 5*, to name two, are versions of this popular design (*Satcom F4* was built by RCA, the other major manufacturer of communications satellites). The HS 376 is cylindrical, like *Intelsat VI*, but only twenty feet long when deployed. When the shuttle launches one, it pushes it out on springs, Wilson told me. The insides of the satellites are then "despun" and a dish-shaped antenna pops up at one end, like the lid of a can. This dish collects signals from the ground, feeds them into an amplifier, and then beams them back down to the ground. Doing this requires surprisingly little electricity. *Galaxy 1*'s twenty-four transponders can transmit twenty-four channels of television at just nine watts each—approximately the same output as a flashlight.

When my tour ended, I turned in my smock and drove over to the Airport Park Hotel to meet Tim Givens and Doug Brown, Jr. Tim and Doug work for a magazine called *STV*, which of course stands for "satellite television." *STV* is an informative publication whose writers nonetheless sometimes stray into the realm of fine writing. "Looking back over many a dull and droll biology course," one editor wrote recently while musing about the proper plural of *antenna*, "we seem to remember that 'antennae' were something on bugs (female bugs at that). Antennas usually are on houses, cars, buses, boats, airplanes and other sundry modes of transportation and places of habitat."

Tim and Doug are not primarily or even secondarily writers. Their jobs at the time I knew them involved driving around the United States and Canada in a van with two dishes (the safest plural of *antenna*) mounted on a trailer behind it. Every four hundred miles they would stop, rev up their portable Honda generator, tune in each of the dozen or so North American birds that carry significant amounts of television, and measure the strength of every channel. Satellites gener-

ally don't transmit their signals uniformly in all directions but
instead focus them on the parts of the earth they want to
reach. *Westar 4*, for example, aims the bulk of its signal at
the continental United States (the best viewing area is somewhere in the Midwest). The area where a satellite's signal falls
is known as its footprint. Doug and Tim's mission was to
measure all the footprints and compile a signal-strength chart
that would help people in different parts of the country figure
out what size dishes they ought to buy in order to receive
good pictures.

I had learned about the Van'tenna (as the vehicle is known)
in a copy of *STV* that I had bought on a whim. I live in Manhattan, where there is essentially no market for private satellite
TV. You just can't put a dish in your apartment, and if you could
you probably wouldn't, because the city is teeming with microwave interference (primarily from the phone company, but also
from taxi radios, beepers, cellular phones, and television relays,
all of which bounce around among the skyscrapers and play
havoc with satellite signals). There is no reason in the world for
my local newsstand to carry *STV*, but it does. In order to keep
the magazine in stock, I stroll in every couple of weeks and buy
another copy, creating the illusion of impetuous demand. On the
cover of the first copy I bought was a picture of the Van'tenna,
its two big dishes filling the foreground. Tim was standing
alongside and looking through the viewfinder of a video camera.
In the background, peeking over the tops of some trees, was
the Washington Monument. When I saw that picture, I knew I
wanted to ride in that van. I called Tim's boss, and he said it
would be all right.

Tim, Doug, and I drove in my rental car up to Reseda,
several miles north of Los Angeles, where they had left the

Van'tenna. Tim and Doug were both in their early twenties and both from Shelby, North Carolina, where *STV* is published. Both had moustaches. Doug had a thick drawl that turned his partner's name into a languorous disyllable: *Teeeeeeeeum.* The van was parked in front of the home of Denis Dushane, who with his two brothers and a third partner owns Janeil Corporation, a manufacturer of dishes, receivers, and other satellite equipment. Denis had a big Janeil dish mounted on a pole above his patio. In his living room was a big-screen TV, a huge bank of electronic equipment, and shag carpeting so thickly padded you could have dived into it from the back of the couch and not hurt your head. We watched a little television with Denis and one of his children, just to get in the mood, and then loaded up the van and headed for San Diego, where the next signal check was to be made.

The Van'tenna is a sleek Dodge Ram painted silver and festooned with racing stripes. Virtually every inch of its surface that isn't covered with a racing stripe is covered with red or blue lettering: CAN-AM '84 CROSS COUNTRY ROAD TRIP SATELLITE TELEVISION FROM COAST TO COAST STV/ONSAT CAN-AM ROAD TRIP. (*OnSat* is a weekly programming guide published by the *STV* people.) The interior of the van is done up in plush gray upholstery and wall-to-wall carpet, most of it installed by Doug. There are little futuristic venetian blinds in the windows. On that trip most of the back of the van was filled with electronic equipment: two MTI 2800 antenna positioners, two Gould satellite receivers, a GBS 2600 satellite television test set, a Sky Eye, a Sky-Angle, and lots of other stuff. There was also perhaps a hundred dollars' worth of pennies that Tim had tossed back there.

About halfway to San Diego we pulled off the road at a

public beach, put our hands in the Pacific Ocean, and walked around aimlessly for a while. We stopped again a little later to watch the sunset. A more or less steady stream of people came over to ask about the dishes. "You get the Playboy Channel on that?" This is a question that almost everybody eventually asks, and the answer to it is yes. A desire to see naked women on their television sets, according to dish dealers, is one of the main reasons men buy dishes. It's not the reason they keep them, however. "They watch the Playboy Channel for about a week," Tim told me. "Then they never watch it again, except when their friends come over and ask them, 'Hey, do you get the Playboy Channel on that?' " A man who looked a little like Barney Rubble came over and said he had been thinking about buying a dish. He and Tim discussed specifications. "You get the Playboy channel on that?" he asked finally, and I stopped holding my breath.

When we were back on the road again, something at Camp Pendleton kept setting off Tim's radar detector. Then we saw a UFO. Ringed with red lights, it zoomed across the sky, stopped suddenly, and swerved off at an impossible angle. What looked like little faces peered down from the windows and seemed to signal us—but it turned out to be just a prank, a helium balloon with a flare tied to it drifting slowly across the sky. At around seven we stopped to buy gas. "It seems weird that back home it's damn ten o'clock," Doug said. Next door to the gas station was a store apparently called the Liquor Motel. We went in and bought scotch, bourbon, and beer.

*T*here are two circumstances in which you are allowed to watch as much television as you want to: when you are sick and when you are at a motel. Most normal people, when they go into a motel room, turn on the television set immediately, even before they go into the bathroom to see what kind of free soap the maid has given them. At our Best Western in Vista, though, we didn't bother with the TV in the room. Tim called the airport to find out our latitude and longitude. Then Tim and Doug began to set up the equipment.

A dish antenna isn't shaped like just any dish. If you sawed one in half, the cross section would be a parabola. Microwaves landing anywhere on a parabolic surface are reflected to a single point above its center. This focuses and amplifies them, making it possible to transform a weak and dispersed signal from outer space into twenty-four channels of television (or as many as 324,000 simultaneous telephone conversations). You can demonstrate this principle by putting your ear at the focus point and listening carefully while Tim and Doug shout "You idiot!" into the dish. The sound waves act just like microwaves from space, bouncing off all parts of the dish and boring powerfully into your brain.

The concentrated satellite signal at the focus point is gathered by a funnellike device called a feedhorn, which strengthens the signal and prunes away unwanted frequencies. The signal is then fed into a low-noise amplifier (LNA), which beefs it up further and passes it along to a down converter, which changes its frequency and passes it on to a receiver, which amplifies it again and passes it on to a radio-frequency modulator, which turns it into exactly the sort of signal a television set is accustomed to receiving from its VHF antenna or cable.

Before a dish can receive a signal from a satellite, it has to be aimed directly at the satellite. Tim aimed our dish by taking the latitude and longitude of our motel, subtracting them from the latitude and longitude of *Comstar D4*, consulting his *World Satellite Aiming Guide* (published by *STV*), yelling at Doug, fiddling with some dials, and yelling at Doug again. Finally he found *Comstar*. Once you know where one satellite is, finding the others is easy. (People whose dishes are installed in permanent locations don't need to go through this rigamarole every time they want to watch TV; most systems have computerized actuators that move the dishes automatically.)

Well, Doug and I had a beer and Tim had some scotch. Then I had some bourbon and Doug had another beer and Tim had some more scotch. Then we all had a drink, and so on. A commercial for LA beer came up on the screen. Low-alcohol beer! What's the point? Then we watched some sort of helicopter show. Tim flipped away from it just as the helicopter was about to be blown up with a Molotov cocktail made out of a camping lantern. I was actually starting to get interested in the show—did it really have a budget big enough to allow for the destruction of a helicopter?—but when you have your own earth station, you don't want to waste all your time watching one particular channel, because there are so many other channels that you could be watching. So Tim moved us over to *Galaxy 1*, where we watched a few minutes of a baseball game.

During the Olympics, Tim said, people with dishes could watch any event that was going on at any time, by flipping through the numerous transponders that ABC had leased for the occasion. They didn't have to watch those girls running around with ribbons if they didn't want to. They could watch those horses running around on the golf course instead. And no commercials. During the 1984 political conventions, he said, he'd seen network correspondents scurrying around the floor, yelling at their technicians, combing their hair, complaining about the stupid politicians, and—mostly—complaining that they weren't getting as much air time as they deserved: network television in its underpants, as it were.

One of the most popular satellite "shows" used to be the Chicago feed of ABC's *World News Tonight.* For several hours each afternoon Max Robinson, the Chicago anchor, would sit at his desk in front of a live camera, preparing for the few minutes during which he would be woven into the fabric of the evening news. While he waited, he yelled at his colleagues, told dirty jokes, screamed at people on the phone, and developed a wide but secret following among dish owners. Dish installers checked out new systems by tuning to the Max feed. Fans built vast libraries of Max tapes. Some people felt that the "hairspray incident" was the purest expression of Max-ness; others savored the continuing series *Max Buys Things on the Phone.* Max cults sprang up. Finally ABC caught on and shut him down.

We poured another drink, and Tim turned to transponder 12 on *Satcom F4*—the Playboy Channel. When I was in third or fourth grade, my friend John Ruth told me that late at night, after the three networks had gone off the air, you could see naked women on TV. This was not the only piece of incorrect information I ever received from John Ruth. But on several occasions when I was spending the night at his house, we stayed up past *Moment of Meditation* and the musical version of the Lord's Prayer and turned the dial expectantly from staticky blur to staticky blur until, finally, at what seemed like dawn but probably wasn't much past midnight, we fell asleep.

Nowadays, however, third and fourth graders in many parts of the country are able to do what John Ruth and I were not. A game show called *Everything Goes* was on the Playboy Channel when Tim tuned in. A young woman was introduced to three men and then had to try to identify them by looking only at their bare bottoms. She missed two out of three and had to let a fourth man take off some of her clothes. She and this man, her opponent, were asked various questions, and when they answered wrong they had to surrender some of their clothes. Finally it was time for the last question, which would decide which contestant would have to take off almost everything. "The guy almost never has to strip," Tim said. Sure enough, the woman was asked an impossible question and had to let the man take off her brassiere. After a full half hour of inane buildup, she didn't seem nearly naked enough. Then she had to stand around—reluctantly, it appeared—chatting casually with the host and the other contestants while the credits rolled.

At ten o'clock the manager of the motel came out and said that the portable Honda generator was making too much noise. No problem! We poured another drink and Tim produced three huge orange extension cords from somewhere in the van. We linked them together and ran them from the van across the parking lot, up over the balcony, and into Tim and Doug's room. We stuck the plug into the wall socket. The picture came back on. We had a drink to celebrate and then flipped to a more pornographic channel. The manager came out again to say that a guest, apparently having stuck his head out his window and focused binoculars on the van's rearview mirror, had discerned that we were watching something that offended him and had requested that we knock it off. No problem! While the manager lingered at the door of the van, eyes glued to the screen, Tim pulled out a sort of vinyl tarp that hooked onto gismos in the ceiling of the van and formed a curtain covering all the windows. By this time we had drunk to what is commonly called excess, and putting up the curtain involved a great deal of falling down and knocking over bottles, cans, suitcases, the ice chest, papers, boxes, tools, and pieces of electronic equipment. Pennies tinkled onto the asphalt. Lights flicked on in a number of motel rooms, and a few doors slammed. We poured another drink and decided that, all things considered, we had watched enough TV. I drained my glass while Tim and Doug shut down the equipment and became hopelessly entangled in the serpentine extension cords. And so to bed.

"*G*inger Rogers did everything Fred Astaire did, except backwards and in high-heeled shoes," said Pat Porter, who had just been introduced as "the most wildest speaker we've ever had." *We* was STTI, Satellite Television Technology International, a trade association made up of people who build and sell earth stations. STTI was holding a trade show, the week before Thanksgiving, at the Loews Anatole, in Dallas. Porter, the marketing manager of a company called StarCom, was giving a talk titled "The Oldest Profession Explained." I slipped out before I could figure out what he meant by this. He couldn't possibly have been referring to the home-satellite business, which is neither old nor a profession (although, like all businesses, it longs to be the latter; some dish dealers have taken to calling themselves certified satellite professionals).

Earlier that morning, in the auditorium where Porter was speaking, a man named Guy Davis had asked, "Is there anyone that's been in the industry for more than two years?" Perhaps ten people, in an auditorium filled with earth-station dealers, distributors, and manufacturers, raised their hands. One of the hallmarks of the earth-station movement is, to put it mildly, a certain thinness of experience. "The uninformed person is capable of making a very good living in this industry," Davis confided. A recent survey, he said, had found that 80 percent of new dish buyers were unhappy with their purchases, presumably because dealers had installed them improperly or made exaggerated claims. "That's a sad statement of affairs to make," Davis said. Even the experts haven't been experts for very long: five years ago only a handful of people had so much as heard of satellite TV.

At one point I stepped out into the hotel's parking lot to take a look at seventy-five dishes of varying sizes, all aimed at the Clarke Belt and funneling television signals into the convention hall. There were supposed to be more dishes, but the parking lot isn't very big. At the previous major satellite show, at Opryland, in Nashville, there had been more than 300 functioning antennas.

Back inside, I wandered past an extortionate hot-dog stand and made my way into the main exhibition area, where several hundred booths had been erected. Television sets were everywhere: *Bewitched*, *The Right Stuff*, the Three Stooges, a tape of the most recent space-shuttle mission, *Regis Philbin's Healthstyles*, the new Paul McCartney video, a program in Spanish called *Principles of Sunday School Growth*, *The Young and the Restless*, a Canadian McDonald's commercial in French, *I Dream of Jeannie*, the Weather

Channel. Two Dallas Cowboys cheerleaders were autographing little plastic footballs at the StarCom booth. When they finished signing a football, they tucked it hygienically into a little plastic bag. I put mine in the pocket of my jacket and moved along to the Basic Systems booth, where Mrs. Texas was autographing pictures of herself. (*Miss* Texas would be on duty at the StarCom booth the next day.) In another part of the hall was Kenda Moore, a volunteer sheriff-dispatcher whose other titles, according to a bulletin she handed me, include Miss Pre-Teen Missouri, Junior Miss Missouri, Camdenton's Junior Miss, Miss Teen Missouri, Miss Camden County, and, most recently, Miss DialCo (DialCo makes mounts for dishes).

The crowd in the exhibition hall was a boot-rich and tie-poor collection of relatively young and almost exclusively white men who gave the impression of having entered the earth-station business after having lost almost all their money selling citizen's band radios. The equipment on display was bafflingly various. There were solid dishes, mesh dishes, fiberglass dishes, aluminum dishes, plastic-coated dishes, stainless-steel dishes, white dishes, black dishes, small dishes, huge dishes, one-piece dishes, two-piece dishes, fifty-piece dishes. One company was selling a dish that could be mounted on the roof of a camper; another was selling one that folded up like an umbrella. "We guarantee it for a year, but we expect it to work fine for five," said one grinning exhibitor, his arm wrapped like a steel band around the shoulders of his would-be customer.

"What makes your dish different from everybody else's?" I asked another exhibitor. "It's blue," he said. A man nearby was selling a polyurethane foam called FrothPak, which he said was a fast-setting alternative to concrete and was suitable for dish-mount installations. He was demonstrating the stuff by squirting it into paper cups, where it looked like that frozen glop sold at 7-Eleven stores. "I used to put straws in them," he said. Every now and then someone came up and tried to make off with one. Exhibitors at two booths were selling videotapes intended to teach dealers how to install satellite TV systems. One videotape recommended doing something that the other videotape said never to do (use electrical tape).

I asked a reporter from a trade magazine how many of these exhibitors he thought would still be in business the following year. "About thirty to fifty percent," he said.

The earth-station industry is going through a period of churning innovation. Rapid technological evolution has made it possible to buy an earth station today for a fraction of what an inferior system cost just a short time ago—but that evolution has also left a lot of corpses. Part of the fun of wandering around a trade show like the one in Dallas lies in trying to guess which exhibitors will end up as forgotten martyrs to the business they are creating. Ominously, several booths were manned by Japanese.

*L*ater in the day two representatives from HBO paid a surprise visit to the Loews Anatole and held a secret meeting with the board of directors of SPACE (the Society for Private and Commercial Earth Stations), a trade association. The chairman of SPACE is Taylor Howard, the engineering professor who built the first American backyard earth station. Shortly after the meeting began, I joined a small group of trade-magazine reporters in geostationary orbit outside. A camera crew from Boresight, a perhaps too hastily named satellite television network that covers developments in satellite television, shot some poignant footage of the closed door.

Actually, everyone knew what the secret meeting was about: HBO's plan to scramble its satellite signals in order to make them unintelligible to backyard earth stations. HBO had announced that it was on the verge of encrypting its programming. This plan greatly annoyed SPACE, STTI, and almost everyone with a dish in his backyard. The fun of owning an earth station would diminish sharply if there was nothing up there to watch, and it was feared that HBO's move would have a domino effect.

The debate over scrambling, and about who owns the microwaves that carry television signals through outer space, is typical of the sort of confusion that arises when technology bounds off in some bold new direction. Americans are accustomed to thinking of television as something they receive for free. Television is part of "the air"; you turn on your set and there it is. Satellite television also comes out of the air, and therefore it should be available to everyone at no cost, according to this way of thinking. There is also a quaint but widespread conviction that things that are invisible are not real and thus cannot be owned. Cable television seems different because it is distributed by wire, and people are used to paying for things that travel by wire (such as electricity and phone calls).

Programming suppliers like HBO take the wholly modern view that a satellite television signal can be stolen just as surely as an idea can. In most other contexts it would be hard for an educated person to argue with this point of view. Germs, oxygen, and many other essentially invisible things

are now known to be quite real. But satellite television poses
a special problem. HBO would not exist if American taxpayers
had not pumped hundreds of millions of dollars into the space
program over the last quarter of a century. Every American
communications satellite has been heavily subsidized by the
public. If HBO had had to pay the true cost of developing and
deploying the technology that its business depends on, an individual HBO subscription might cost—who knows?—
$100,000 a month. Earth station owners argue that it is the
programming suppliers who are being naive. The owners see
television from space as the first real return on their substantial investment in astronauts and rockets. They say they don't
mind if the programmers scramble, so long as backyard earth
station owners are given some means of decoding, and paying
for, the services they want to watch.

If such a system of paying for premium programming is
ever established, it will almost certainly amount to a death
sentence for Direct Broadcast Satellite (DBS) television. DBS
is the system under which several companies plan to use high-
powered satellites to transmit original programming directly
to subscribers equipped with small dishes. DBS was conceived
early in the satellite television era, when equipment was still
primitive and dishes had to be large in order to pick up acceptable signals from the low-powered satellites then in existence. The belief at the time was that the only way to make
dishes smaller and cheaper, and thus attractive to a large
market, was to build bigger, more powerful satellites. Guided
by this belief, several companies committed hundreds of millions of dollars to the construction of such satellites in the early
1980s.

Exactly what, if anything, these satellites will eventually
be used for is now in doubt. Improvements in earth-station

technology have made it possible for small, cheap dishes to pick up clear signals from old-fashioned low-powered satellites, rendering the big birds irrelevant.

All of this is enough to make one marvel at the sleek efficiency of that old-fashioned mechanism for underwriting television: commercials. Yikes!

*K*enneth Schaffer said, "There are two hundred and sixty-six million people in Russia watching this, and only, let's see, two, three, four, five"—he was counting the people in the room—"six people in America." This was an exaggeration of course; most of the people in Russia were asleep.

We were huddled around a television set in a cramped room at Columbia University's W. Averell Harriman Institute for Advanced Study of the Soviet Union, watching the test pattern of Programma I, the principal Soviet domestic television network. "This is the most beautiful test pattern in the world," Schaffer said, as pleased as if he had created it himself. We were watching it live, by satellite.

Soon the test pattern was replaced by the face of a clock, which ticked down the last few minutes to show time. It was three minutes before four o'clock in the afternoon in New York, which meant that it was almost eight in the morning on the shores of the Sea of Okhotsk, where Programma I's broadcast day was about to begin. (Several more hours would pass before the network came on in Moscow, where it was almost midnight. The Soviet Union extends across eleven of the world's twenty-four time zones.) The clock gave way to a fluttering red flag, and it was time for the news. The graduate students at Columbia call this show *Good Morning Siberia*.

Tuning in to Programma I in the United States is extremely complicated. Soviet television is technically quite different from American television, and you can't watch both with the same equipment. Furthermore, Programma I isn't carried by a Clarke Belt bird. It's transmitted by four nongeosynchronous satellites, called Molniya 3s, which are spaced ninety degrees apart in a high elliptical polar orbit. Every few hours Programma I goes off the air for several minutes so that Russian downlink operators can shift their forty-foot dishes from the Molniya that is fading out to the Molniya that is fading in.

This seemingly clunky system actually has many advantages for the Russians. Nearly a quarter of the Soviet Union is so far north that it can't be "seen" by a Clarke Belt satellite: the curve of the earth gets in the way, even from 22,300 miles up. A Molniya, by contrast, can see virtually all of the Northern Hemisphere from the highest point in its orbit. This orbit is also less expensive to achieve than a geosynchronous one. The Soviet practice has been to launch lots of big, cut-rate, rattletrap satellites and replace them as they fall apart. That usually doesn't take very long. The Russians have orbited about a hundred Molniyas in the twenty years they've been using them to transmit television.

The Molniya orbit looks very strange on a map. Its perigee, or lowest point, is just 600 kilometers above a spot in the Southern Hemisphere, and its apogee, or highest point, is more than 40,000 kilometers above Hudson Bay. (Because each Molniya satellite takes twelve hours to travel around the earth—half the time it takes the earth to turn on its axis—it actually makes two loops each day. Twelve hours after the Hudson Bay apogee it reaches another one, over central Siberia. Only the Hudson Bay apogee is used for television transmission; the Soviets use the Siberian one for voice and data transmission.)

As a Molniya approaches its apogee, its apparent motion in relation to the earth decreases, just as a distant airplane seems to move more slowly than a near one flying at the same speed. During this portion of its orbit the Molniya appears from the ground to be almost stationary for several hours, making it easy to aim at. Arthur C. Clarke refers to the Molniya orbit, affectionately, as "the Anti-Clarke Belt."

Despite the considerable peculiarities of the Russian system, Western satellite hobbyists began picking up bits and pieces of Programma I in 1979. Ivariably some crucial elements of the transmission would be missing—the color and the sound, for example. But it was genuine domestic Russian TV, the same thing that average Soviet citizens were watching, and it was live.

Early in the 1980s Kenny Schaffer began to think he might be able to build a system that would pick up more than fragments of Programma I. Schaffer, a chain-smoking former rock-and-roll publicist (for Alice Cooper, among others), was recently described by *Electronics Week* magazine as an "inventor and philosopher of science." He has dark curly hair, a Groucho Marx moustache, a manic verbal delivery, and fifteen hundred hours of unreleased Jimi Hendrix tapes, which he acquired while working on a posthumous Hendrix album. Schaffer is a sort of aging hippie entrepreneur whose principal remaining link to the Woodstock era is a tendency to forget to patent his inventions. These include the first workable wireless microphone and the first wireless electric guitar, which he developed in 1977. His customers—before other manufacturers learned to duplicate his unprotected transmitter and receiver—included not only the Rolling Stones, Kiss, the Electric Light Orchestra, and Pink Floyd, but also Bell Laboratories, the Jet Propulsion Laboratory, and NASA, which used his technology to improve space communications.

By 1983 Schaffer figured he had just about licked the Molniya problem. Despite the objections of his landlady, he was picking up Programma I with a rudimentary tracking antenna mounted on the roof of his apartment building. He began trying to persuade several large universities to hire him to build full-scale systems for them. But the universities were skeptical; most engineering professors didn't believe that he could do what he said he could, and Sovietology professors weren't interested. In the end only Columbia took a chance on him.

Columbia's system, which Schaffer installed in the fall of 1984, consists of a sixteen-foot dish, an Apple computer programmed to track the satellites automatically, a commercial microwave receiver, a modified French-format Sony television monitor, Schaffer's (patented) "d-Cyberia" audio decoder, a modified video-cassette recorder, and several other pieces of customized equipment. Soviet television has better color and higher resolution than American television. When Schaffer first turned on the monitor for a test, Jonathan Sanders, the assistant director of the Harriman Institute, was flabbergasted: the picture was better than the one he was used to seeing on his own TV.

On the Siberian news the day I stopped by Columbia someone was addressing the Supreme Soviet. Like most Russian orators, this man rumbled along soporifically, seldom lifting his eyes from his text. It began to seem possible that his speech would last until the end of time. The camera occasionally cut to the audience, whose members were solemn and heavy-lidded; all they had to keep them awake was the prospect of voting unanimously in favor of whatever it was that was being said. Later there was a report on the disaster at the Union Carbide plant in Bhopal, India. The newscast ended with the weather lady: -17, -22, -9, -14, -15, -19, -3, -5, -1, -6. If for no other reason than that, it was nice to be an American that day.

Programma I doesn't have a rigid schedule. The news ends when the newsreaders run out of news to read. On some days they finish in ten or fifteen minutes; on others they go on for more than an hour. After the credits had rolled, we moved on to the morning exercise show, a great favorite at the Harriman Institute. A muscular man and woman grimly marched in place, to the accompaniment of a piano. Their expressions were sober and ideologically correct, although both occasionally permitted themselves small smiles. The graduate students knew the exercises by heart: "This is the duck dance." If Jane Fonda and Richard Simmons had suddenly walked onto the set, all four exercises would have vanished in a flash, matter and antimatter colliding.

At last it was time for what the students call *Million-Ruble Movie*. That day's offering was the second half of a Lithuanian suspense film, *Collision*. As in virtually all Soviet movies, the colors were muted and earthy—no bright reds or blues, no razzle-dazzle. But the cinematography was skillful and really quite beautiful. After about fifteen minutes, though, the film suddenly stopped, cutting off one of the actors in mid-word. Was something wrong? No. DEAR COMRADES, said a sign on the screen, WE DECLARE A TEN-MINUTE TECHNICAL BREAK. The sound track switched to loud, fast music, with lots of ringing bells. It was meant to wake up the Siberian downlink operators, who had to stop snoozing long enough to move those big antennas.

A few minutes later the movie came back on (the picture was sharper—the first Molniya had been ailing) and the actor finished his word. *Collision* is set in a hospital. Several doctors were walking around in surgical gowns. They looked just like American doctors, with one peculiar difference: their noses stuck out over the tops of their surgical masks.

The students at the Harriman Institute have picked up a lot of interesting trivia about the Soviet Union by watching Programma I. A few weeks before my visit they had discovered that Russian drivers keep their windshield wipers in their glove compartments. When it starts to rain, the drivers pull over and attach the wipers. When the rain stops, they pull over again and remove them. It seems that a rubber shortage a number of years ago prompted someone to steal wipers from someone else, who then stole some from someone else, and so on, until windshield wipers in glove compartments became part of Russia's cultural heritage. The students have also learned that people and wheat almost never appear together on the Russian television screen. Wheat doesn't grow very tall in the Soviet Union, and in order to play down this fact the wheat harvest is usually filmed with no recognizable reference point (a day seldom passes on Programma I without a story about wheat or tractors or both). The camera is held down close to the ground, to make the field look like a forest. Harvesting equipment is shown only from a great distance. But every now and then, the Harriman students said, you can see a farmer standing in the background, the amber waves of grain lapping at his knees.

Later on we watched a *Nova*-like documentary about a

brave new technological breakthrough. In an apartment complex in Moscow, the narrator explained, an elite group of scientists was conducting an exciting experiment. The camera focused on a control box mounted on a wall. Then it followed some wires down into the basement. Then there was an interview with an expert in a white lab coat. The documentary, it turned out, was about automatic heat control. Thermostats, comrades! Still later we watched another scientific program, a popular series whose name means, roughly, *Believe It or Not* (a literal translation, one student said, would be *Obvious and Unbelievable*). That episode concerned an ancient scientist whose name was recognized by no one in the room. He was slumped in a chair. "He has one book on his table always," intoned the narrator. *"Faust."* The camera regarded him protractedly, as though waiting for his last words. The show was completely believable and incredibly boring.

But ours was a privileged tedium; we were the only people in America watching live Programma I. This wouldn't be true for long. Schaffer was holding discussions with other potential customers, including several universities, the United States Information Agency, the Defense Department, and the Soviet Embassy ("Everybody wants to watch hometown telly," Schaffer said). And he was planning to take his show on the road. He had rigged up a Molniya tracking system on a trailer and was offering colleges the chance to book an evening of live Russian TV. He was also planning an even more ambitious international-television project: a system that will pick up live transmissions from fifteen countries simultaneously and display them on a bank of monitors arranged in a semicircle. A viewer will be able to stand in the middle and watch the world.

"It's rock 'n' roll," Schaffer had told me earlier in the day.

"It's electronics, it's media, it's peace. I don't care about 'peace' peace; that's a software concept. I'm just talking about having the opportunity for an error." Like many Schaffer pronouncements, that one was fairly cryptic. (After a certain point in our lengthy interview, which I nonetheless enjoyed enormously, I stopped changing the tape in my recorder and simply turned the same cassette over and over.) But I know more or less what he meant. He sees satellite television as an instrument for global understanding. ("I have to pay back for Alice Cooper.") No country, not even the Soviet Union, can seem entirely foreign once you've gotten to know its weather lady. This is why Schaffer is eager to sell his tracking system to the Defense Department. Even if military planners start out thinking of their dish as nothing more than a piece of spy equipment, he says, in time they'll learn what the students at the Harriman Institute have learned: that life in the Soviet Union, though different from life in America, is still life. Schaffer doesn't ask that the planners forget about the missiles in Russian submarines. But the world would be a safer place, he believes, if every once in a while they would also think about the windshield wipers in Russian glove compartments.

Arthur C. Clarke lives in Sri Lanka. He put a dish in his yard in 1975, but it blew over. This wasn't a big loss. There hadn't been anything to watch except one channel of Indian television, which had been devoted mostly to Indira Gandhi. By 1983, though, the programming available on satellite had improved, and Robert Cooper, the publisher of *Coop's Satellite Digest*, got to thinking that the man who had conceived of satellite television ought to be able to watch it. So he organized an expedition to put a new dish in Clarke's yard.

Clarke is a mystical presence in the world of satellite TV. "There are these gravity wells around the planet," John Zelenka, one of the people who went along on Cooper's expedition, told me. "There are some places over the equator where the earth's gravity is so strong that satellites placed there don't need fuel, because they never drift off position. It turns out that one of the most stable places on the planet is directly above the piece of property that Arthur bought in Sri Lanka. It makes you wonder where this man came from."

Zelenka works for a New York company called Star Video, which, among other things, installs commercial antenna systems and provides uplinks and downlinks for business teleconferences. He has green-and-purple-tinted glasses and a gold earring. Like Kenny Schaffer, he came to satellite television from the world of rock 'n' roll. He was a guitarist and a sound technician before he installed his first dish, for Nelson Doubleday. The Doubleday installation was touch and go. Zelenka didn't quite know what he was doing. He'd never actually seen a dish before Doubleday's arrived. But finally he figured that he had everything right, and he went inside to test the system. He turned on the television set. There was static, then a picture. It was *2001: A Space Odyssey*, the Stanley Kubrick movie based on a story by Arthur C. Clarke.

"It seems likely that the twenty-four-hour orbit will be of fundamental importance for the future of world communications," Clarke wrote in 1956. It's astonishing to think that until very recently "variety" on American television consisted of three indistinguishable networks broadcasting three indistinguishable schedules. Satellite-fed cable TV has often been criticized for failing to live up to expectations: most of the new channels, people complain, aren't very interesting. But in comparison with what was available before, the lineup these days is dramatically various. Gavel-to-gavel coverage of Congress, news around the clock, the weather, rock 'n' roll, most of Boston College's 1984 football schedule, *Fútbol Internacional*, life aboard the space shuttle, Japanese variety shows, the New York Stock Exchange ticker, recent movies, *The Brady Bunch*, naked women. None of it is terribly profound, but neither is most of life.

Watching satellite television probably won't be as much fun in the future as it has been over the past few years. Probably all the premium services will eventually scramble their signals, and the networks will probably scramble most of their feeds. No more Max Robinsons. But maybe someday a cable system will follow Kenny Schaffer's suggestion and offer Programma I to American viewers. Or maybe Mexican television will catch on in Canada. Satellite television has made the world a little cozier; the globe is shrinking under the Clarke Belt.

"I'm totally sold on Arthur," Zelenka says. "Communications satellites have made space a place."

Splace.

(1985)

VI.
THE FIFTH ESTATE

"*I*f the bird is tame," Freud wrote, "I like to place him on a stand and then, while telling him what a good bird he is, I get behind him and lift one of his feet. . . . Birds which are not tame will generally require handling by two individuals with one holding the patient in a towel and the other doing the cutting."

There's a lot more to it than that. I'm just touching the major points. Before trying this yourself you'd want to read Arthur Freud's entire article, "Proper nail clipping of birds," in the January issue of *PSM*. *PSM* is a magazine for pet store owners. Its name stands for Pets Supplies Marketing. Say that aloud a few times and you'll understand why they use only the initials.

Let's see. On August 4, 1984, nearly 300 people in Las Vegas stood up and said, "Bowling belongs in the Olympic Games, and I pledge that I will do everything I can for that goal," according to *Bowling Proprietor*. The bowling industry's Olympic aspirations are "rapidly becoming the talk of the town," the magazine says. Still, bowling linage was down a bit in 1984. Perhaps hoping to reverse that trend, residents of Indiana last year contributed $296 to B-PAC, the bowling political action committee. B-PAC tries to entice politicians to adopt a more pro-bowling stance. One of its beneficiaries is my own congressman, Bill Green, of New York City, whose district contains exactly one bowling alley.

Here are a few of the magazines that are piled up on the table in my dining room: *Turkey World, Iron Age, American Carwash Review, National Jeweler* (edited by S. Lynn Diamond), *Fur Rancher, Lab Animal, Hosiery & Underwear, Weeds Trees & Turf* (incorporating *Golf Daily*), *Infections in Surgery, American Cemetery.* I also have *Kitchen & Bath Business, Ground Water Age, Beverage World* (the average American drank 43.2 gallons of soft drinks in 1984), *National Mall Monitor, Quick Frozen Foods, Lodging Hospitality, Hardware Age, The National Notary* ("Only in Florida, Maine and South Carolina may Notaries join couples in matrimony"), *Meat Plant, Pulp & Paper, Pizza Today,* and a couple of hundred others.

Although according to my wife it is now impossible to sit down in our apartment without sitting on a copy of *Cemetery Management,* my collection of trade and professional magazines is really just the tip of the iceberg in terms of what's available. Standard Rate and Data Service's directory of business publications, which comes out monthly and is larger than the Manhattan Yellow Pages, has more than 5,000 entries. The largest single publisher is Harcourt Brace Jovanovich, whose hundred or so titles include *Plastics Focus, Pit & Quarry,* and the brand-new *Food Sanitation.* Though little known outside their fields, such magazines can be enormously profitable. Last year Rupert Murdoch bought twelve of Ziff-Davis's trade magazines, including *Meetings & Conventions* and *Aerospace Daily*, for $350 million.

Rupert Murdoch notwithstanding, most trade publications don't attract much public attention. When people talk about "the media" they are usually not referring to *Laundry News*. In fact, aside from the 15,387 people who receive it every month, how many Americans are even aware that there is an entire publication devoted to laundry? (Actually, I see in this month's Standard Rate and Data directory that there are several others, including: *American Coin-Op, American Drycleaner, American Laundry Digest, Clean Scene Quarterly, Coin Launderer & Cleaner, Coinamatic Age, Drycleaners News, National Clothesline, New Era Laundry & Cleaning Lines, Textile Maintenance Reporter,* and *Western Cleaner & Launderer.*) The specialized focus of most trade magazines gives their editors a certain privacy: They can speak to their readers with a candor that is impossible in the popular media. One could never find out from reading *Time* or *Newsweek*, for example, that people who make pretzels are considered to be somewhat boring by people who make potato chips. This is a fact that to the best of my knowledge can be found in print nowhere except in the pages of *Snack Food*.

Before I started piling up trade magazines, I had a vague, free-floating sense—derived mostly from watching the evening news—that there were only about a dozen different jobs in the United States: my job, Dan Rather's job, the president's job, steelworking, farming, banking, law enforcement, driving taxis, several others. But now I realize that the economy is almost inconceivably various and that in addition to the occupations just mentioned there are also jobs involving, for example, the building of clam bunk skidders, the marketing of feller-bunchers, and the repairing of log forks (*World Wood*). I also know that 42 percent of men believe they have sensitive skin (*Progressive Grocer*) and that the 1973 Arab oil embargo, though disastrous for almost everybody else, was just about the best thing that ever happened to the people who make chain saws (*Chain Saw Age*, not to be confused with *Chain Store Age*).

Trade and professional magazines make some of the most esoteric reading in the world. They are the forum where American business talks to itself. Flipping through them is like eavesdropping on private conversations.

*I*f keeping up with all these magazines didn't take so darned much time, I might be tempted to start a magazine of my own. It would be a sort of compilation of the best parts of all my favorite trade and professional publications. I wouldn't be able to call it *Magazine Age, Communication World,* or *Editor & Publisher,* because there are already magazines with those names. Perhaps I would call it *The Other Media* or *The Fifth Estate.* It would be filled with page after page of arresting facts. For example:

> "Coffee aroma consists of 100 to 200 volatile chemical compounds derived from the thermal degradation of primarily sucrose in the process of roasting the coffee bean." (*Tea & Coffee Trade Journal*)
>
> "Astronaut Sally Ride's recent space mission not only advanced the space program, but also prosthetic dentistry. Material used to make her urinary catch device is

now being used to make soft denture liners." (*Dental Management*)

"Some people call it polish. Others say class. We term it professionalism. Trying to sum up just what professionalism is, is somewhat like trying to define beauty or honesty. It's either there, or it isn't, but its presence adds a very special luster. And Uniforms by Mindy has it." (*Uniforms & Accessories Review*)

"Ironically, Notaries are rarely seen in modern American dramas and musicals—although this nation has more Notaries than any other and their role is an important one. The reason is that the office of Notary is viewed as an auxiliary rather than a primary vocation in modern America (except in Louisiana, with its French heritage), and characters are identified by their primary vocations— as in Arthur Miller's 'Death of a Salesman.' " (*The National Notary*. This may be the most self-absorbed magazine in existence. An article in a recent issue explained that Vanessa Williams lost her Miss America title because she "violated the morals provision of a notarized agreement.")

"There is always money waiting for those who can 'master the earwaves.' " (*Waterbed*)

"Under current [Mississippi] state law, coroners are required only to be registered voters of the county in which they reside and never to have denied the existence of a Supreme Being." (*Morticians of the Southwest*)

"Finally, combining the edible with the collectible, Freelance will introduce Goofy Pops (TM), a lollypop on a 'squiggly straw.' The candy will be wrapped in a cellophane which will have a puffy sticker with rolly eyes attached to it. Extra stickers will come with the Goofy Pop." (*Giftware Business*)

Every now and then, my magazine would cover certain stories in greater depth. I might, for example, consider running an entire article about Goofy Pops, which in the taxonomy of giftware are classified as "stationery." (So are Mello Smello Mini Duffles, stick-on Mello Smello scratch-and-smell tattoos, Wild & Wacky Mello Smellos, Smell & Spell fragranced message stickers, and Smellopads.)

Stationery is a category of giftware, but it isn't the same thing as a *gift*. Before I started reading *Giftware Business*, I was a little confused on this point. Now I understand that a gift in the giftware sense isn't something like a fishing rod, a set of golf clubs, or anything else you wish someone would give you. Rather, it is something like a pewter figurine of a scuba diver, a tiny panda sculpted from "hydrostone," a pencil sharpener in the shape of a monkey standing in a shoe, or a ballpoint pen packaged with a color-coordinated ladies' bow tie.

One place where people buy a lot of giftware (according to a recent issue of *Souvenirs & Novelties*, a magazine whose readership overlaps somewhat with that of *Giftware Business*) is the souvenir shop at the Oklahoma City Zoo. (Another place is the gift shop at almost any hospital. In fact, hospital gift shops have their own trade magazine, called *Hospital Gift Shop Management*.) In an article entitled "Zoo Shop Employees Create Functional Displays," Judy Rowe, manager of the zoo shop, explains the secret of her success: "When someone walks in and asks for something penguin- or tiger-themed, we'll show the shopper whatever is currently in stock. We don't stop after showing one item. I prefer to take a few extra moments and make sure my customer is aware of everything—the plush, statues, and pictures." *Plush* is the giftware word for fuzzy stuffed things. According to *Giftware Business*, teddy bears led the plush list last year, "but lambs did pick up momentum."

The line between gifts and souvenirs is thin. Souvenirs are generally a bit less inhibited: a baseball cap covered with golf-ball-sized plastic peas and a huge plastic pat of melting butter; "underwear that's funtawear" from British Bulldog LTD; toilet paper imprinted with sayings like "Show business is my life"; a pair of hat-wearing Maw and Paw 'Zarky Doodler Hillbilly Character Pens sold in a "2-holer outhouse display-gift package"; Famous Amish Dolls; fake tomahawks made by Cherokee Indians from North Carolina ("We're on the warpath to bring you fast selling items that bring high profits for you!").

Cherokee tomahawks aside, gifts and souvenirs tend to be made on islands in the Pacific. This sometimes causes tension. An article in *Souvenirs & Novelties* discusses the perceived indelicacy of selling Japanese-made souvenirs in American battleship museums. The problem can usually be overcome. "In the past three years I have had only one person who, after discussing this issue, still refused to buy," reports Hattie Horton, retail manager of the gift shop at Battleship Alabama Memorial Park.

If you just bought up your local battleship museum's entire supply of Bother Me greeting cards (for example, "It bothers me when you eat with your mouth open") but don't have anyone in particular you want to send them to, you might consider buying a mailing list consisting of the names of, say,

all the people who between January and August of 1984
bought the phonograph record *Floyd Cramer Piano Favorites*, "featuring World Famous Love Songs and a Treasury of
Favorites." There are fifty-nine thousand such people, 90 percent of them female. Finding out who they are costs fifty dollars per thousand names.

Selling names and addresses is a very big business. Popular lists, according to recent issues of *Direct Marketing* and
Fund Raising Management, include people in the state of
California who have rented or purchased wheelchairs, canes,
walking chairs, or crutches; women who subscribed to *Red-
book* after responding to a sweepstakes offer; members of the
Association of Handicapped Artists; Americans "concerned
about the growing Soviet military threat to peace"; buyers of
the Thompson Chain Reference Bible; buyers of the Perry
County Pizza Kit; and "people interested in the welfare of
children and who support building character, teaching valuable skills, providing adequate education and suitable housing,
along with developing networks to help abused, lost, stolen
and abandoned children." (Another popular mailing list consists, apparently, of the names of people who subscribe to
magazines dealing with popular mailing lists. Shortly after I
began reading *Direct Marketing* and *Fund Raising Management*, I received a piece of junk mail urging me to purchase
three books by someone named Cecil C. Hoge, Sr.: *Mail Order
Survival and Success*, *Mail Order Know-How*, and *Mail Order Moonlighting*.)

*F*or a couple of summers when I was in college, I worked
as a reporter for a trade magazine called *Milling & Baking*

News. Shortly before I went to work there, the magazine had come to something resembling national prominence by breaking the story on the famous "Russian wheat deal," the Soviet Union's enormous purchase of American grain in 1973. For several weeks that year, Walter Cronkite, *The New York Times*, and the rest of the popular media relied on *Milling & Baking News* for virtually all their information about the transaction. This information was uncannily accurate. The magazine's editor, Morton I. Sosland, was getting it from an anonymous source who, Sosland gradually realized, was probably a Soviet official. (The source always addressed Sosland as "Mr. Morton," something American Deep Throats wouldn't do.) Excitement about the wheat-deal story had mostly died down by the time I signed on, although work in the office was still occasionally interrupted by a British or Japanese television crew looking for an offbeat American feature story.

As is true of many trade publications, *Milling & Baking News* has a tiny circulation—just a little over 5,500. Even so, the *Wall Street Journal* once described the magazine as being "indispensable" to its industry. Its influence derives not from the number of people who read it but from who those people are. About a fifth of the magazine's readers are the chief executives of milling or baking companies. Most of these people read every issue carefully, and advertisers pay a premium to reach them. A full-page, full-color ad in *Milling & Baking news* costs about $2,500. That's not much money in absolute terms, but it works out to nearly half a dollar per subscriber, or about what it would cost to read the ad aloud to each one over the phone. A similar advertisement in *Time*, by contrast, has a cost per paying reader of less than three cents.

It is a general rule that the more carefully a trade magazine is read by its trade, the more stultifying its content is to outsiders. Indispensable or not, *Milling & Baking News* is pretty grim reading for anyone who doesn't care deeply about milling and baking. "In the face [of] sharply higher prices last week," begins a typical article in a recent issue,

> shortening business was very sluggish. Soybean oil for nearby jumped 2½ @ 3⅛c a lb on the heels of 1¼c gain the previous week. Deferred prices rose 1⅛ @ 3⅞c. Virtually all other oil varieties also were considerably higher. Loose lard finished up 1½ @ 2c and edible tallow gained 3½c. . . .

The magazine can keep this up for pages and pages. Still, trade writing is not without its charms. *Milling & Baking News*'s use of the symbol "@" in place of a hyphen in price ranges is, I believe, unique. The *News* is also the only publication I know of that consistently uses the word *firm* correctly. Most business writers treat *firm* as a synonym for *company* or *corporation*. It is not, in strict usage. A firm, according to *Webster's Third New International Dictionary*, is "a partnership of two or more persons not recognized as a legal person distinct from the members composing it." Editor Sosland—who once had a brand of flour named after him ("Bigboy"), also maintains an idiosyncratic but absolute ban on the word *however*.

As a summer intern at *Milling & Baking News*, I wasn't qualified to write the dense grain-market analyses that are the heart of the magazine (although I was once allowed to contribute an editorial praising an astronaut who had smuggled a sandwich into outer space). My usual beat was much humbler: obituaries, new product announcements, rewritten press releases. Most trade magazines depend heavily on press releases, often reprinting them verbatim. It was always a matter of pride at *Milling & Baking News* that a press release was never run without our at least switching around the order of the clauses and changing all the *he stated*s to *he said*s.

New product announcements are the most fascinating part of almost any food-related trade magazine. "*Ex-Cel*, a microcrystalline cellulose powder, adds bulk to food products without adding calories," the January issue of *Prepared Foods* reports. "When mixed with water, *Ex-Cel* forms a ribbon paste ideal for low-calorie spaghetti, macaroni and other formed products." Another issue of the same magazine announces "a fluid, oil-based coloring" ingredient that "yields a butter color on popcorn or extruded snacks." Butter color has what the prepared-food industry calls "eye appeal." A closely related concept is that of "mouthfeel," as in, "Our formulary explains how to use Avicel MCC [another cellulose bulking additive] to make a coleslaw dressing with controlled flow, cling, and improved creaminess without sacrificing high-fat mouthfeel." (Eye appeal and mouthfeel are often difficult to improve without sacrificing yet another desirable quality, "consumer labeling appeal.")

Some of the most popular new products are ones that enable food manufacturers to replace expensive ingredients. "HOW TO MILK CHOCOLATE" reads the headline on an advertisement in *Candy Industry* for Durkee's line of "coating fats," "cocoa butter equivalents," and other chocolate extenders and substitutes. A similar product is Viobin Cocoa Replacer, which, according to an announcement in the January issue of *Food Technology*, "is made from defatted wheat germ and 5% added carbohydrate which is pressure toasted to a rich brown.

It is then ground to a fine powder which is similar in color and texture to processed cocoas."

Even better than new product announcements are patents for new processes and ingredients. Here are a few garnered from recent issues of *Food Technology:*

U.S. 4,472,592. . . . Process for producing a meat-based product having a meat core of substantially constant cross-section of relatively dense compacted meat and an outer coating of fat which is mobile in the uniform state.

U.S. 4,466,476. . . . Method for converting salmon green eggs into a roe product in which the green egg is agitated in a saturated aqueous solution of salt containing a nitrite to impart a scarlet color, after which the salted egg is dried and agitated in a saturated aqueous solution of a malate containing sufficient nitrite to impart scarlet coloring.

U.S. 4,478,861. . . . Method of preparing a frozen food product in which a plurality of cooked pieces is treated to remove free water to form voids after which food mass is subjected to a freezing gas to surface freeze pieces while leaving some unfrozen moisture thereon. Dry powder additives are then introduced with agitation to uniformly coat pieces, after which they are fully frozen throughout and transferred to a storage container for later reconstitution.

Most people probably think they would never eat a frozen food product in which a plurality of cooked pieces had been treated to remove free water to form voids. But in fact almost everybody cheerfully eats stuff like this. Much of the food in modern restaurants traces its ancestry directly to the patents page of *Food Technology.* "Pre-cooked," "pre-browned," and "portion controlled" frozen food items are simply "microwaved" and either "plated" immediately or, in the fancier establishments, gussied up with inexpensive "profit-makers" like olive bits or almond slivers before being "menued" as expensive "signature" entrees. There isn't much need for chefs anymore. Kitchen technology has advanced to the point where a pre-browned slice of portion-controlled prime rib can be microwaved in a minute or two and then kept in a holding oven for either hours or more without losing eye appeal.

"*E*ye Appeal," according to an advertisement in the January issue of *The Director*, "is still the main reason people buy!" The ad is for "Aurora's new 18 gauge 1500 shell with accent stripes. . . . This new ACCENT series features a stripe on the top and base moldings that color coordinates with the shell finish. Notice how the interior shade completes this color combination. The striping has been market tested and found to be widely accepted." The ACCENT series also features "adjustable bed, seam welded bottom, metal gimp and material-lined foot end."

Aurora is the Aurora Casket Company of Aurora, Indiana. *The Director* is the official publication of the National Funeral Directors Association. Food-related publications are a lot of fun, but for pure, bone-chilling enjoyment there's nothing like a funeral magazine. *The Director, Casket & Sunnyside, American Funeral Director, Stone in America* (gravestones, that is), *Cemetery Management, Morticians of the Southwest, American Cemetery, Southern Funeral Direc-tor*—if I had to choose a single trade magazine to accompany me into an 18 gauge 1500 shell, it would probably be one of these.

"Silver Taupe with Ash Grey Crepe interior, it does sound exciting, doesn't it?" asks Gene C. Hunter, the president of the Marshfield Casket Company, in a recent issue of *Morticians of the Southwest.* "More families are wanting caskets with new interior designs that are different and stand out over others."

A modern casket is a remarkable piece of merchandise. It is the single most expensive piece of furniture that many people will ever own, yet its only real function is to be lowered into the ground and covered with dirt. Its numerous optional features serve no purpose except to increase the final bill. With racing stripes, or plain? How firm a Sealy mattress? Should the interior upholstery coordinate or contrast with the exterior finish? Persuading grieving relatives to purchase these unnecessary amenities is known to the trade as "loading the casket." It is the mainstay of the funeral business.

Many expensive casket features are seemingly meant to prevent or delay what has already occurred. Batesville caskets are treated with "an exclusive Chemgard coating" intended to add "additional protection," according to advertisements in various funeral magazines. Marshfield's premium Signature caskets (the Monarch Blue, the West Coast Blue, and the Silver Taupe) offer a "one-piece rubber gasket" and a "50-Year Warranty." Belmont's Bronze Masterpiece caskets are protected by "a lustrous 4-millimeter, twice-baked, hand-rubbed Dupont finish" applied over a generous coat of "Dupont Adhesion Promoting Primer." Batesville's Sapphire, Mediter-

ranean, and Tourmaline models have both inner and outer lids,
the better to protect a loved one from—well, from what?

Loading the casket doesn't stop with the casket. Most
caskets, even ones with two lids, aren't buried in the ground;
they're buried in other caskets, known as vaults. Wilbert's
Monticello, Continental, Venetian, and Triune models (with
their Strentex and Marbelon liners) all provide "the very finest in underground protection." According to an ad in *The
Director*, Wilbert tests these vaults in an "immersing tank"
that subjects them to

> a side wall force of over 18,000 pounds at a depth of
> twelve feet. In another test, a freeze/thaw machine takes
> Wilbert burial vaults to temperatures of 30° below zero.
> And Wilbert's instrumented burial vault provides accu-
> rate technical data from a Wilbert burial vault buried at
> a normal depth, through sensing devices attached to an
> external digital readout device.

Sozonian's top-of-the line vault is made of twelve-gauge steel
and "designed like a real I-Beam to give it plenty of self-
supporting strength"; optional " 'Electro-Shield' protection" is
also available.

Another profit maker for funeral directors is burial clothing. "A Thing of Beauty, a Joy Forever" is the motto of Wil-
lingham Tailoring Company, manufacturers of funeral dresses
and jobbers of burial underpants. Morticians can also order
the second revised edition of *Desairology: Hairstyling for the
Deceased*.

It's all an elaborate ripoff. And yet, these magazines are
fascinating, no? The best of them is *American Funeral Director*, a monthly journal that contains, in addition to adver-

tisements for caskets, vaults, burial clothes, and other paraphernalia (including SnFF, the nonformaldehyde arterial
chemical that "has no smell!", and King Tut, the popular cav-
ity fluid from Egyptian Chemical & Funeral Supply), articles
with headlines like "LUNG CANCER IN WOMEN UP 152.6% IN
TENNESSEE," "FIND BONES IN ATTIC," and "JOB-RELATED
DEATHS HIT RECORD LOW IN '83." (I've got some good news
and some bad news.) A chart in the February issue reveals
that Hawaii, Nevada, Rhode Island, and South Dakota suffered no weather-related deaths in 1983, while Texas led the
nation, with sixty-six. Like all good trade magazines, *American Funeral Director* is obsessed with its subject; unlike most
trade magazines, it has a subject that lends itself to obsession.

Reading the funeral magazines can be a peculiar experience. They make mortality seem simultaneously vivid and unreal: vivid because nothing could be more vivid than a bottle
of SnFF; unreal because you can almost begin to believe that
the color of the inside of your casket is something that might
one day make a difference to you. As Freud wrote, "No one
believes in his own death."

That's the other Freud, incidentally—the one who didn't
know anything about birds.

(1985)

VII.
THE MUSEUM
OF FAILED PRODUCTS

A nice frosty can of Sweat would certainly taste good right now. That's Pocari Sweat, a popular Japanese soft drink. The naming of beverages is yet another area in which the United States lags behind Japan (where Sweat shares shelf space with Yogut, Sour White, and Fruit Calpis).

The can of Sweat that I am contemplating at the moment is not actually for sale. It is part of a display at the International Supermarket and Museum, in Naples, New York. The museum is the creation of Robert McMath, the chairman of Marketing Intelligence Service Ltd., a consulting outfit that tries to keep its clients abreast of worldwide developments in packaged goods. McMath is a tall, graying, good-natured man who says he personally sees about 70 percent of all the new products introduced in America each year. His museum (which is open only to MIS clients) is a sort of shrine to the best and worst in marketing.

"Being a Scotchman, I never throw anything away," says McMath. He means that literally. The museum, which is located in a restored nineteenth-century granary, looks like a cross between an art gallery and a grocery store. It displays about five thousand items on a rotating basis. (McMath has tens of thousands of others stashed in another building.) Among them are disposable "denim" diapers, microwave browning spray, and bug-killing window cleaner from South Africa. McMath and his staff of twenty-one constitute a sort of Platonic ideal of unfettered consumption: simply not having something is enough to make them buy it.

The mainstay of MIS's business is *Product Alert*, a "weekly briefing on consumer product introductions throughout North America." The publication logs the arrival of new items and occasionally attempts to place them in a larger historical perspective. When Strutzel Products of Chicago recently introduced a beverage called Watermelon Soda, *Product Alert* noted the existence of a precursor: "an old line of 'Mickey's Melon' soda using watermelon as the flavor—Mickey Rooney's favorite." MIS also publishes more specialized reports and conducts seminars for clients. According to McMath, "A client will come to us and say, 'We want to know what's going on in the dry mix business, not including baking mixes. And we'll say, 'Okay, here are two thousand different products from the last seventeen years.' " McMath's desk is invisible beneath a mountain of index cards. MIS's newest venture is CAT*TRACK, an ambitious service that employs two hundred fifty free-lance shoppers to sleuth out new products in the United States and seventeen foreign countries. Swedish toilet paper rolls, one learns, are among the largest in the world; Brazilian rolls are among the smallest.

The most arresting part of the museum is the section devoted not to new products but to failed ones. Eighty percent of all new products never make it past the test-market stage, McMath says, and some of the most forlorn losers end up on the shelves at MIS. One of McMath's personal favorites is Touch of Yogurt shampoo, a doomed extrapolation from the dairy case, but there are many runners-up: Gorilla Balls vitamin-enriched malt candy; I Hate Peas ("A Potato and Pea Recipe in French Fry Form"); AfroKola ("The Soul Drink℠" and "The Taste of Freedom"); Nullo deodorant tablets; Yogurt Face & Body Powder ("contains a large amount of living yogurt culture and high quality smoothing ingredients"); Male Chauvinist "awfully arrogant aftershave" and "outrageously superior cologne"; Gimme Cucumber hair conditioner; Hair Trigger shampoo; Sillyclean mirror cleaner; Snack in the Mouth creamy freezer pops; Top Coverage hair-colored spray paint for bald spots (still sold to a loyal few); Northwoods Egg Coffee; Mister Meatloaf; Baker Tom's Baked Cat Food ("the *only* cat food that is actually baked in an oven the same way you bake at home").

In truth, the difference between a new product and a failed one is sometimes difficult for a layman to discern. Coffee in tea bags failed; so did tea for instant coffee makers. Why didn't Chocolate Styling Gel? Why can you still buy I.T. cheese spray ("One can of 'instant taste' will flavor more popcorn than 4 lbs. of butter") but not Finger Frosting? The gods of marketing are fickle and inscrutable. I felt a small pang when I discovered a can of Silly String displayed ignobly among the losers. Silly String was a sort of pink, extruded, plasticky material that sprayed out of an aerosol can. You could sneak up behind your mother and blanket her with a great linguinelike mantle of bubble-gum-colored gunk. This is no longer possible, although making Jiffy Pop is. Why?

Some failed products may have failed simply because they were ahead of their time. In the early 1970s, Gerber guessed correctly that busy young adults would be attracted to foods that could be prepared in a hurry. But Gerber packed its entry ("Singles") in baby food jars. The nation's singles, already grumpy about having no one to eat with, drew the line at dipping their spoons into tiny jars of creamed beef and Mediterranean vegetables. Pokems ("The neat drink in a bag," each sold with its own poking straw) looked an awful lot like those popular juice drinks now being sold in aseptic containers. But poking a Pokems was a bit like stabbing a water balloon. The promising new product soon went the way of Captain Cat cat litter deodorant.

Other products disappeared no doubt because they didn't live up to the expectations they raised in the minds of consumers. Wine & Dine Dinners, instant meals packaged with their own miniature bottles of spiced-and-salted cooking wine, sold briskly to people who thought the wine was for drinking but who *(yuck! ptui!)* quickly discovered otherwise and never bought them again.

Walking through the aisles at the New Product Museum, one quickly develops a sense of the implacable optimism at the heart of free enterprise. Parsnip Chips, Moonshine Sippin' Citrus, Secret Valet Bathroom Deodorizer and Tissue Roll Holder—somebody once had high hopes for each of them, as high as Procter & Gamble's hopes for Pampers. Meetings were held, strategies were promulgated, consultants were consulted. The first cases rolled out with fanfare and enthusiasm, and—and nobody paid any attention.

Robert McMath's collection of failed products also makes it clear that American consumers have more self-control than is commonly assumed. For the most part, it is true, we buy what the people on television tell us to buy. When we were told to buy cheese-flavored cat food, we did. When we were told to buy cat food in numbered cans, we did. But when we were told to buy cat food that had been *baked*, we said, "Enough!"

(1985)

VIII.
COPIES IN SECONDS

A friend of mine called not long ago to ask if I would send him a copy of a certain newspaper clipping. I said I would. I rooted around in the stuff on my desk and found the clipping near the bottom of a big stack of papers. I moved it to the top and made a mental note to take it to the drugstore across the street, which has a coin-operated photocopier. Because I don't work in an office, I can't just run down the hall and make a few thousand free copies of a clipping, a recipe, my hand, a newsy Christmas poem describing my family's heartwarming experiences during the previous year, or anything else.

Several days passed. Every time I went out I either forgot about the clipping or remembered it and decided not to do anything about it. If there's anything I hate, it's carrying around a large, loose, irregularly shaped piece of paper while I do various errands. If someone had grabbed me by the cheeks and told me to march right over there and make that copy, I would have replied, like Bartleby, "I would prefer not to." I toyed with the idea of retyping the entire newspaper article—a pleasant way to spend an afternoon. Gradually the distance between my apartment and the drugstore grew in my mind to the point where it might as well have been the distance between St. Louis and the moon.

Then early one morning as I lay sleepless in bed, I came to the sudden, powerful realization that I would never make that copy unless I made it on one of those little personal copiers that Jack Klugman is so enthusiastic about on television. The necessity for making large expenditures often comes to me in such a flash. I now believed, in other words, that walking across the street to spend twenty cents for a single photocopy was less convenient and more irrational than driving across town to spend several hundred dollars on an entire machine that I would then have to find a permanent place for in my apartment.

Well, the next day I drove across town to a discount electronics store and bought a Canon PC-10 personal copier for $475. (This was quite a bargain; the manufacturer's suggested retail price was $795.) Canon personal copiers use special cartridges that contain, as Jack Klugman says, "the entire copying process." These are sold separately. I bought two for about $50 each. I also bought five five-hundred-sheet packages of ordinary bond paper, which were on sale for a total of just $15.

A Canon personal copier is very small—about the size of two toaster ovens—but the box it comes in is very large—about the size of six or seven toaster ovens. Maneuvering the box and the cartridges and all that paper up to my apartment turned out to be quite a problem. I finally made it, though, and set up the machine without much trouble. I put the clipping on the platen, inserted a sheet of paper, and watched a crisp, clean copy emerge from the other end.

A feeling of well-being and deep inner satisfaction coursed through my veins and arteries. My life had achieved a sleek new efficiency. I could now enjoy in my own home a pleasure usually known only to people who have real jobs. "So long, sucker" I imagined myself saying to the man who runs the drugstore across the street.

I made another copy of the same clipping and threw away the first one. Then I made a third and threw away the second. Then after a panicky moment in which I wondered whether I had not just satisfied my copying needs in their entirety, I opened up the owner's manual and began, page by page, to copy that.

*E*ven in the days when I hated making copies, the ability to do so was something I took for granted. Much of journalism consists of photocopying things that other people have written and finding slightly different ways to write them again. Obviously, this has not always been possible. Twenty-seven years ago Jodi Stutz could not have lost her job at Deere & Company, in Moline, Illinois, as she did in 1980, for making a Xerox copy of her bare bottom, because twenty-seven years ago Xerox office copiers did not exist. Until relatively recently, making facsimiles of ordinary business documents was so difficult and expensive that almost no one bothered to do it.

The first office copiers were, as is well known, monks. When Gutenberg invented movable type in the early 1400s, monkdom trembled. Sometime afterward the Abbot of Sponheim wrote a lengthy treatise arguing that monks "should not stop copying because of the invention of printing." To ensure that his treatise got the readership it deserved, the Abbot had it printed. A couple of hundred years went by. In the mid-1600s someone pressed a moist piece of tissue paper against a written document, causing some of the ink of the original to transfer to the tissue. A couple more hundred years went by. Blueprints were invented in 1842. Typewriters, carbon paper, and mimeograph machines were introduced a few decades later.

Carbon paper and mimeograph machines were improvements over hand copying, but neither could be used to reproduce documents that already existed. Mimeography, furthermore, was a terribly inefficient way to make a small number of copies, since each document required its own master. Schoolchildren love mimeograph copies, because they smell so terrible, but almost everyone else hates them. Photostat machines, which were introduced in the early 1900s and which made copies photographically on sensitized paper, were much too expensive for ordinary office use. They were also too big, too slow, and too hard to use. When a businessman needed a copy of something, he generally called in the functional equivalent of a monk.

This didn't really begin to change until the middle of our century, five hundred years after Gutenberg. In the early 1950s, the Minnesota Mining & Manufacturing Company (3M) and Eastman Kodak introduced office copiers called, respectively, Thermo-Fax and Verifax. Both were small and inexpensive. Their chief drawback was that they made dreadful copies. Thermo-Fax used a heat-sensitive paper that tended to continue darkening long after it had left the machine. Verifax produced copies that were even stinkier than mimeographs. Neither machine made copies that were archival, or permanent. Both machines required special paper, which over time cost users a fortune.

Office copying as we know it didn't arrive until 1960. That was the year when a small company in Rochester, New York, began marketing its Haloid XeroX 914 Office Copier (the second capitalized *X* is a flourish that the company later dropped.) The 914, unlike its competitors, made good, permanent copies on ordinary paper. The machine, though large, was simple enough for a child to use. The Haloid Xerox Company (which had started life as the Haloid Company and is known today as the Xerox Corporation) had been marketing a small number of machines employing its revolutionary copying technique for a decade, but the 914, the first model intended for general office use, was also the first to catch on in a big way. The number of copies made in American offices grew from around 20 million in 1955 to 14 billion in 1966 to approximately eleventy zillion today.*

It is often interesting to speculate what life would be like if some conspicuous element of it were removed. Suppose, for example, that the universe contained no solid material that

----

* Some of the statistics in this paragraph are made up. According to the public relations office at Xerox, the world made 522 billion copies last year on xerographic machines sold by Xerox and its competitors. No one really knows the exact number, though, because many copies don't get counted. No one, for example, has called me to ask how many copies I have made of the credit cards in my wallet (three), so world estimates are short by at least that number. The Xerox Corporation makes more copies each year simply in testing its machines than the entire world made for all purposes thirty years ago.

was also transparent—no glass or plastic or anything similar. Without such a substance we would have no windshields, no light bulbs, no contact lenses, no (good) aquariums, no television sets, and so on. What would we do? The loss of xerography—as the plain-paper copying process that Xerox introduced is known—would be less dramatic, but its impact would still be profound. We would have no *Pentagon Papers*, fewer lawyers, more secrets, larger forests, more (fewer?) bureaucrats, less espionage, shorter cookbooks, better memories, fewer cartoons on our refrigerators, and a lot less information in general. Xerography places rapid mass communication within the reach of almost anyone. To see how potent and indeed subversive such a capability can be, one need look no farther than the Soviet Union, where copiers are more closely guarded than computers.

The Xerox machine has given ordinary people an extraordinary means of preserving and sharing all sorts of information. And yet, we take it for granted. The usual cure for this sort of neglect is to focus obsessive attention on the subject for a short time and then never think about it again. This is what I intend to do.

*M*ost people spend more time thinking about how photocopiers don't work than about how they do. "Call key operator" and "Check paper path" have become familiar modern imperatives on a level with "Fasten seat belt" and "Shake well before using." It is commonly believed that the stubbornness of many photocopiers results from the same declining attention to quality that makes the present in all respects worse than the past. But this is not the case. A xerographic copier is a marvel of extremely intricate engineering that, like the post office, actually works much better than one has any right to expect.

Every photocopier that uses ordinary paper employs some version of the basic xerographic technology embodied in the Haloid Xerox 914. At the heart of this technology is a specially treated surface, usually in the shape of a cylinder, that is known as the photoreceptor. In the 914, the photoreceptor was made of the element selenium. Like a balloon that has been rubbed against a wool sweater on a cold day, selenium is capable of holding an electrical charge. Unlike a balloon, selenium is capable of holding this charge only in the dark. If you shine a light on a charged piece of selenium, the charge will vanish from every part that is illuminated.

If you shine that same light on a printed page so that an image of the page is reflected onto a charged selenium drum, the drum will retain its charge in those places where no light falls (that is, in those places corresponding to the dark ink on the page) and lose it everywhere else. If you then sprinkle the drum with an oppositely charged powdered ink, the ink will stick to the charged parts of the selenium surface, in the same way that house dust sticks to a staticky balloon. This produces, on the surface of the drum, an exact mirror image of the original printed page. The drum rolls over a piece of paper, transferring the image to it. The copy is made permanent by a device called a fuser, a small heater that melts the powdered ink and binds it to the page.

A small, unrepresentative minority of readers will undoubtedly write in to claim that they thought of just such a process back in 1930 or so and would I please ask Xerox to send along a royalty check as soon as possible. These readers, though valued as subscribers, must be dismissed as crackpots. Xerography is unusual among inventions in having been conceived by a single person. There was no one in France or Russia who was working on the same thing. The Chinese did not invent it in the eleventh century B.C.

The inventor of xerography was a shy, quiet man named Chester Carlson. For a full decade electrophotography, as he called the process, was his very private obsession. No one took him seriously except his wife. All of the twenty-one major corporations he approached expressed a total lack of interest, thus passing up a chance to manufacture what would later be called, more than once, the most successful commercial product in history. So persistent was this failure of capitalistic vision that by the time the 914 Office Copier went into production, the original patent covering its internal processes had expired.

*C*hester Carlson was born in Seattle in 1906. His mother died of tuberculosis when he was seventeen. His father was an itinerant barber crippled by arthritis. The family moved briefly to Mexico for therapeutic reasons and then for financial reasons settled in a remote and impoverished corner of California's San Bernardino Valley, where Carlson was sometimes the only student in the local school. He worked his way through junior college and then through the California Institute of Technology, from which he graduated with a degree in physics. After college he worked for a short time as a researcher at Bell Telephone Laboratories. He ended up in the New York patent office of a small electronics outfit called P. R. Mallory & Co.

"In the course of my patent work," Carlson said in the early 1960s in a short Xerox film, "I frequently had need for copies of patent specifications and drawings, and there was no really convenient way of getting them at that time." Specifications had to be retyped and then proofread for errors; technical drawings had to be sent out of the office to be copied, at great expense, on a Photostat machine. Carlson often wished aloud that there were a simpler method. When none presented itself, he decided to invent one.

Carlson approached this task with an unrelenting single-mindedness that one would not hesitate to label lunacy had the outcome been different. Perhaps it was lunacy even so. For many months he spent spare moments at the New York Public Library, poring over fat technical volumes. He concluded early on that his copying device, whatever it turned out to be, would have to depend on a process "that used light to affect matter in some way." This process could not be photography, he reasoned, because photography was too well understood and had attracted too many well-financed researchers. If photography held the answer, he would not be the one to find it.

One day in the course of his reading Carlson came upon a property called photoconductivity. The electrical conductivity of certain materials, he read, can be affected by exposure to light. Only a very small handful of materials behave in this way. One of them is sulfur. Carlson bought some at a chemical-supply store and tried to liquefy it by holding it over a burner on the kitchen stove, his principle piece of laboratory equipment. The sulfur caught fire and filled his apartment with a cloud of noxious fumes.

Chester Carlson became quite well known in his apartment building. The odor of rotten eggs drifted under his door and permeated the hallways. Small explosions rocked the walls. One day a young neighbor dropped by to complain. Carlson managed to charm her, and she later married him. Somewhat reluctantly the struggling inventor surrendered two of the burners on his stove.

Married life being what it is, Carlson soon gave up the other two burners as well. He moved his laboratory into a small apartment in Queens owned by his mother-in-law. He also hired an assistant, an unemployed German physicist named Otto Kornei. Carlson couldn't afford to pay very much, but Kornei had no other prospects. For several years Carlson had been performing his experiments without success. Now, with Kornei's assistance, he began to make some progress. The two men coated a metal plate with sulfur. Then Carlson wrote the date and place—*10–22–38 Astoria*—in black ink on a glass slide. He rubbed the sulfur-coated plate with a cotton cloth to give it an electrical charge, placed the slide against it, and held them beneath a powerful lamp for a few seconds. He then removed the slide and sprinkled black powder on the plate. Much to his astonishment, a blurred image of his inscription appeared. Hands trembling, Carlson pressed a piece of wax paper against the plate and then peeled away the world's first xerographic copy.

Carlson was elated; Kornei was depressed and disappointed. The little piece of waxed paper didn't look like much to him. (It didn't look like much to me, either, when I saw it in its display case at the Smithsonian Institution.) Fond of Carlson but concerned about his future, Kornei soon accepted a job offer from IBM.

Carlson spent the next five years tinkering with his invention and trying to find a company that could appreciate its potential. IBM, RCA, and General Electric, among others, turned him down. Finally, in 1944, at the end of his wits and the bottom of his bank account, he was led by a chance conversation to the Battelle Memorial Institute, a private research foundation in Columbus, Ohio. Battelle offered to spend $3,000 developing his idea in exchange for 75 percent of future royalties. Carlson happily agreed and began to spend his spare time in Columbus. The next year his wife divorced him.

*I*n 1945 the Haloid Company earned about $100,000 manufacturing photographic paper and related supplies in Rochester, New York. This was small potatoes and seemed even smaller, because one of Haloid's closest neighbors was the Eastman Kodak Company. Many Haloid employees believed that Kodak could put them in the poorhouse at any moment and that its failure to do so was a sign less of charity than of indifference. Tired of playing sandlot ball in the shadow of a big-league team, Haloid's top management developed a keen interest in finding another line of business.

One day John Dessauer, Haloid's chief of research, noticed a brief account of Chester Carlson's discovery in a technical journal. Electrophotography sounded promising, so he persuaded Joseph C. Wilson, Haloid's president, to accompany him to Columbus for a demonstration. Wilson, an inspired executive who occupies a nearly deific position in Xerox's corporate memory, was impressed. (Wilson died in 1971, at the age of sixty-one, while having lunch with Nelson and Happy Rockefeller in Manhattan.) Early in 1947 Haloid

agreed to support Battelle's research in exchange for the right
to manufacture products based on it. Haloid's commitment
taxed the company's limited resources, but Wilson and his
lieutenants were more excited by copiers than they were by
photographic paper.

Haloid introduced its first xerographic copier in 1949.
(The word *xerography* was coined by a classics professor at
Haloid's request; it is based on Greek words meaning "dry
writing.") This first copier was called the Model A or, more
familiarly, the Ox Box. It was a sprawling, awkward device
that actually consisted of three separate machines. The selenium photoreceptor was not a drum, as in the 914; it was a flat,
heavy plate. The operator had to hoist it from one machine to
the next and repeat the entire time-consuming process for
every copy. The operating manual was filled with dire instructions:

> Dry the plate surface by striking it lightly and briskly
> with a clean, dry, UNTOUCHED portion of cotton. . . .
> With a spoon, carefully spread one-fourth of a teaspoon
> of Xerox Toner over the developer. . . . When mounted
> in the process tray, the four tabs of the electrode should
> protrude no more than approximately 1/64" above the
> level of the side gaskets, nor should they go below the
> side gasket.

Haloid shipped out several Model A's for field testing. All
were quickly returned. "Too complicated" was the verdict.
The machine might have disappeared altogether, and taken
Haloid with it, had it not serendipitously turned out to be an
excellent and inexpensive maker of paper masters for offset
printing presses.

(Offset printing is almost impossible to understand. It is based on the principle that oil and water don't mix. You can make a simple offset press by taking a smooth stone and drawing a picture on it with oil; dipping the stone in water, which will adhere to the bare stone but not to the oily image; dipping the stone in a non-water-soluble ink, which will adhere to the oily image but not the wet stone; rolling a rubber roller across the stone, thus transferring the inky/oily image from the stone to the roller; and rolling the same rubber roller over a piece of paper, thus transferring the image from the roller to the paper. In an offset press using a xerographic master the stone is replaced by a piece of paper and the oil is replaced by a powdered ink that repels water. Before xerography came along, offset masters had to be made using a complicated photographic process.)

A handful of other clunky xerographic products followed the Ox Box over the next decade. All found narrow applications and small but adequate numbers of devoted users, but none was the compact, automatic office copier that Carlson and Haloid dreamed of. Work on this machine proceeded alongside the other projects, but progress was slow.

"Xerography went through many stages in its development at which any sane management committee would have been justified in turning it down," a Battelle staffer said later. "There always had to be something extralogical about continuing."

Carlson continued to contribute to the development of his invention, first as a frequent visitor at Battelle and later as a consultant at Haloid. Rapidly, though, the responsibility for realizing his vision was transferred to others. When the 914 took off, his royalties made him a wealthy man. Carlson retired to his house in Pittsford, New York, where he and his second wife pursued an interest in Eastern religion. He died in 1968.

Whenever John Rutkus came to the Haloid Company in 1955, his first assignment was to make himself a desk. Money was scarce in those days. All available resources were being pumped into the development of xerography. Rutkus was an engineer. He took a hammer and nailed down the wobbly top of an old drafting table.

Rutkus's second assignment was to create a rough design for the machine that would eventually become the 914. The original goal at Haloid was to build an office copier that would be small enough to sit on a desk. It soon became clear that this goal would not be attainable. The copier that began to take shape on Rutkus's drawing board was more nearly the size of a desk. A large desk.

Blocking out the internal design of the 914 required a great deal of imagination, because almost none of the systems that would constitute it had been perfected, or even conceived. The research and engineering departments worked side by side, inventing the machine as they went along. For example, Haloid was determined to build a copier that used cut sheets of paper. This produced enormous problems. Xerography involves the creation of an effect similar to static electricity, and when a piece of paper comes in contact with a charged photoreceptor, it sticks like wallpaper. How to peel it off? Vacuum systems didn't work, because they tended to slurp up the powdered ink. Mechanical grippers marred the delicate surface of the drum. One day, while pumping up a child's bicycle tire in his garage, Rutkus was inspired. He stuck a piece of paper to the hood of his car and blew it off with the bicycle pump. He conceived of a system in which tiny nozzles would lift the leading edge of each sheet with puffs of air. The idea was incorporated in the machine.

Haloid didn't have enough money to build custom parts for its preproduction models. Bolts, springs, and pieces of old cars were scavenged from a junkyard on Clinton Avenue, in Rochester. The plan for the 914 called for a photoreceptor drum about eight inches in diameter. The engineers tried welding sheets of metal into cylinders and coating them with selenium, but they couldn't get the selenium to stick to the welds. At the junkyard one day, an engineer stumbled over a length of discarded aluminum pipe. He took out his tape measure. The outside diameter was eight and a half inches. He bought ten feet, took it to a couple of brothers who ran a small machine shop nearby, and had them tool it down. The pipe was cut into short lengths, coated with selenium, and installed in the machines.

Another problem was the powdered ink, or toner: no one knew how to make one that would work. Haloid's toner plant was nothing more than a drafty old garage on Avis Street. (The optical group was located in the basement of a Masonic temple.) People who worked there went home each night looking like coal miners. The 914 required a toner that would fuse with paper at a low temperature, because heat destroys the conductivity of selenium. Avis Street periodically came up with promising batches, but then the engineeers would change the design of the fuser and hand down a new set of specifications. Sizing was also a problem. New batches of toner frequently contained large, anthracitic chunks, referred to by the engineers as charcoal. When a piece of charcoal got into a machine, it ended up as a smoking blob in the middle of a piece of paper. Often it also wrecked the photoreceptor. The head of the toner group complained that the engineers were making impossible demands, but finding an acceptable formula was a do-or-die proposition. "If we hadn't accomplished the lower-melt toner," Rutkus said later, "we wouldn't have had a product." In the meantime Haloid simply proceeded on the assumption that a suitable toner would be found.

Producing toner was one problem; getting rid of it was another. Nearly a third of the toner that forms each image remains stuck to the photoreceptor after a copy is made. This residue has to be cleaned away. With the Ox Box, cleaning had to be done manually, by rocking the selenium plate back and forth in a tray filled with diatomaceous earth—a pale, claylike powder composed of the remains of tiny organisms. (Early models had used coffee grounds, soybean meal, flax seed, and corn meal; all attracted mice.)

The 914 was going to be fully automatic, so a different method had to be used. The designers settled on a rotating fur brush. Beaver and raccoon pelts were tried and rejected. The belly fur of Australian rabbits, it was discovered, worked just about right. The brushes had to be trimmed to a very tight tolerance: if the fur was too short, it wouldn't clean the drum; if it was too long, it would mar the surface. The engineer who supervised final production of the 914, Horace Becker, took a rabbit pelt to a local furrier named Crosby Frisian and asked him if he could trim it to the proper length, give or take a sixty-fourth of an inch. Frisian's business was making fur coats. He took the yellow tape measure from around his neck and said, "Show me what a sixty-fourth is."

Even after the toner problems had been solved, the 914 was prone to burst into flames. If paper didn't move through the fuser fast enough, it caught on fire. Haloid's early copiers had contained fire extinguishers that kept the heat away from the drum and held damage to a minimum. The engineers began to design a similar system for the 914. Work proceeded apace until the marketing department found out. Fire extinguishers in an office machine? They were incredulous. *Fire,* which had always been a problem with xerographic machines, was a word that did not cross their lips. When they discussed it at all, they called it *scorching*. Black smoke and orange flame could be billowing from a machine and the Haloid repairman would scratch his head and say, "Hmmm, there seems to be a little scorching here." At last a compromise was reached. Fire extinguishers were included, but they were called scorch eliminators.

*N*ear the end of its harrowing effort to develop the 914, Haloid suffered a momentary failure of nerve. The company had no manufacturing facilities to speak of. Demand for its early copiers had never been large enough to require anything so grand as a factory. As the day of reckoning drew near, Joseph Wilson decided that he owed it to his stockholders to explore less risky methods of bringing the 914 to market. He invited IBM to consider a joint venture. IBM hired Arthur D. Little, an old and distinguished management-consulting firm in Boston, to determine just exactly how large the market for an office copier might be.

Haloid had already conducted an impromptu study of the same question. A couple of young salesmen had traveled to several Northeasten cities and asked people in various businesses how many copies they used. Thermo-Fax and Verifax were already on the market, so people had begun to develop a sense of what office copiers could do. In Philadelphia one day, one of the salesmen stopped by the local Social Security office, which used one of the new coated-paper machines.

"How much of that paper do you use?" he asked.

"What do you mean—how many carloads, or what?"

The Haloid man's eyes lit up. *"Carloads?"*

The consultants from Arthur D. Little came to a very different conclusion. The copier Haloid was building was far too large and far too expensive to find a market, they said. The nation's total demand, now and in the future, could be satisfied by a maximum of five thousand machines. "Model 914," their report concluded, "has no future in the office copying market." IBM politely declined to become involved.

Haloid's executives swallowed hard but elected to go ahead. The first production model rolled off the assembly line in 1959. "Rolled off" is literally correct: The first 914s were assembled on wooden pallets with wheels on them. When a worker finished with his part of the machine, he pushed it to the next station. The pallet could be tilted sideways so that the copiers, which were the size of deep freezes and weighed more than six hundred pounds, could be squeezed through doors.

Demonstrating the 914 was difficult. Only a few of the machines existed (at first the factory turned out just five a day), and they were too big to tote around. The solution, Haloid decided, was television. The company had now spent so much money that spending even more was eerily euphoric. The 914 commercial, which first aired in 1960, showed a businessman at a desk.

"Debbie, will you please go make a copy of this?" the man asks a little girl.

"Okay, Daddy," she says.

"That's my secretary."

Debbie goes skipping off and copies the letter by pressing a single button. A voice explains that the 914 makes a first copy in less than a minute and produces seven copies a minute after that. Debbie scoops up the copy, turns, stops, and goes back to make a copy of her doll.

"Thank you, Debbie," her dad says. "That was fast. Which is the original?"

Debbie looks at the paper and scratches her head. "I forget!"

From the vantage point of the nonstop 1980s, it is almost impossible to believe how long a sixty-second commercial seems to last. Still, the Debbie spot and several other major promotional efforts were phenomenally successful. An angry competitor demanded proof that Debbie was not a midget; how could a child operate a machine like that? Haloid, which by now was well on its way to becoming the Xerox Corporation, very nearly found itself with more business than it could handle. The company's revenues grew from $32 million in 1959 to $60 million in 1961 to more than $500 million in 1966. A ten-thousand-dollar investment in Haloid stock in 1960 was worth more than a million dollars by 1972.

"*T*he more you understand about xerography," Robert Gundlach says, "the more you are amazed that it works." Gundlach must be more amazed than anybody, because no one understands the subject better than he. At last count he held

131 patents, most of them involving xerography. (He has also
invented a snow-making system, a sundial, an unusually com-
fortable backpack, and a 20,000-volt electrostatic generator
that can be manufactured for just five dollars.) Gundlach
wasn't officially involved in the development of the 914; by the
time that project got under way, he was hard at work on the
machines that would follow it. But when members of the 914
team had problems, they went to him. More often than not he
had a solution.

Like many gifted inventors, Gundlach seems to have been
spawned by alien beings. When I met him at the 914's induc-
tion into the Smithsonian Institution in 1985, he was wearing
light blue pants, a light blue plaid jacket, a light blue striped
shirt, and a light blue tie with some sort of large bird painted
on it. He is tall, gaunt, and tanned—like a rancher. In his
office at the Xerox research facility, outside Rochester, he has
a small smooth stone that he likes to spin on the surface of his
desk. When he starts it going counterclockwise, it spins along
smoothly for a while, then begins to wobble. All of a sudden
it reverses direction and spins the other way.

When I first saw this I wondered whether Gundlach had
not just inadvertently revealed an interesting fact about his
planet of origin. But it turns out that the spinning stone has
a terrestrial explanation. The stone is asymmetrical. When it
spins counterclockwise, it starts to vibrate, converting rota-
tional energy to translational. This somehow causes it to reverse direction, making it appear to violate the law of conser-
vation of momentum.

Gundlach's father was also an inventor. His one patent
was for Wildroot Cream Oil. When he made his first batch,
he put it in a tube, anticipating Brylcreem by many years.

Executives at Wildroot, where he worked, didn't like it; they thought it looked like toothpaste. He spent a few years in bitter disappointment. Then the Second World War depleted the nation's supply of alcohol, the principal ingredient of Wildroot's bottled hair tonic. Gundlach's invention was alcohol-free. He added a little more water to it, so that it, too, could be poured from a bottle, and resubmitted it. This time the executives loved it. Reminiscing in his office, Robert Gundlach began to sing: "You'd better get Wildroot Cream Oil, Charlie, start using it today, something, something Cream Oil, Charlie, chasing all the girls away." As a teenager, he spent a summer standing over a large vat in Buffalo, mixing all the Wildroot Cream Oil in the world.

One of Gundlach's most important contributions to the 914 was helping to solve its paper-handling problems. "I had a friend who took physics with me," he once said. "Every time we went into an exam he said, 'Force equals mass times acceleration and you can't push a rope. That's all you need to know about physics.' " You also can't push a piece of paper through a Xerox machine; you have to pull it. In addition to the problems involved in unsticking paper from the photoreceptor drum, there were equally tenacious problems involved in sticking it on in the first place. The 914 had to handle all kinds of paper, from card stock to onionskin, and it had to handle them in all climates and humidities. Paper in New Orleans is soggier than paper in Cincinnati, and it behaves differently in the machine. Different kinds of paper have different kinds of grain, which affects how and whether they will curl. Curl added in one part of the process has to be subtracted in another. The way paper is cut during manufacturing puts a burr on the edges, which makes it difficult to separate one sheet from another. And so on.

Gundlach went into semi-retirement this year. He had reached retirement age, and he needed to pick a date. He selected January 15—exactly thirty-three and a third years, one third of a century, since he had joined the company. He was too valuable to let go entirely, so Xerox offered him a small staff and his own laboratory, where he still works three days a week. Many of his current efforts are directed at enabling Xerox to enter the very-small-copier market, which is dominated by the Japanese, should it ever decide that it wants to.

*T*he Japanese are a constant source of concern at Xerox. Not far from Gundlach's office is a sort of museum of competing copiers, most of them built by Japanese companies. The man in charge of this collection is Hal Bogdonoff. Like the commander of the unit of the United States Army that stands in for the Russians in war games, Bogdonoff has so thoroughly immersed himself in the minds of his adversaries that he now thinks more like them than like his employer. Ask him about a new Xerox product, and he confesses ignorance. Ask him about someone else's machine, and he can describe it from the screws up. His group conducts detailed autopsies of other companies' products, carefully analyzing each new feature and making precise estimates of manufacturing costs.

Among the first things one learns upon tearing apart other people's machines is that there is really no way to make a copy on plain paper other than the way that Chester Carlson invented. There have been a great many advances in xerography over the years, but every machine on the market today takes as its starting point Carlson's original patents. Those patents gave Xerox an extraordinary competitive advantage in the 1960s. Carlson had worked in a patent office, and he knew how to protect an invention. Xerox's monopoly lasted until the 1970s, when the last of the early patents expired.

Xerox's grip on the copying market was tested in three major lawsuits in the 1970s. First Xerox sued IBM for patent infringement. Then, in 1972, the Federal Trade Commission sued Xerox for violating antitrust laws. The next year SCM Corp. sued Xerox for the same thing. All three suits dragged on for years, in part because the invention of xerography had made it possible for lawyers to turn pretrial discovery into an open-ended orgy of photocopying. Xerox eventually prevailed in the IBM and SCM suits, but a 1975 settlement with the FTC required it to give its competitors licenses on its office-copier patents.

Xerox did not handle its first taste of real competition with much aplomb. The company's salesmen had been accustomed to sitting around all day with their feet on their desks, waiting for the phone to ring. Now their customers discovered that they had alternatives. In addition, Xerox's breakneck growth in the 1960s had largely destroyed the extraordinary fraternal spirit that had enabled a rinky-dink local company to transform itself into one of the most powerful corporations in the world. In the early days there had been no separation between the research and engineering departments; a discovery by one was savored by both. Now product development was snarled in bitter bureaucratic rivalries. Meanwhile, the Japanese prospered.

It is greatly to Xerox's credit that it responded to these difficulties not with demands for tariffs and trade restrictions but with a full-scale rethinking of the way it did business. The company began to pay attention to its customers.

It also threw out its old manufacturing system and built a new one on the Japanese model, cutting costs in half. Today Rochester is one of the few cities in the United States that has a positive balance of trade. Copiers assembled at the Xerox plant in Webster, just beyond the city limits, are shipped directly to Japan, where they have done well in a tight market. Here at home, in spite of increasingly stiff competition from the Japanese, Xerox's share of the copier market is actually growing.

Partly because Xerox has been so successful, employees speak of their company's competitors with open admiration. Canon in particular has emerged as a powerful and innovative force in xerography, not only in its tiny personal copiers but also in its larger machines. When I paid my visit to Webster, Bogdonoff and his staff were especially impressed by an "intelligent" Canon copier that they were dissecting in their laboratory. In place of some of the usual lenses and mirrors, the Canon contained a "charged couple device array," a computer chip that converted light into digital information. This information can be stored in memory or transmitted to a laser scanner. The machine can take one image, blow it up vertically, shrink it horizontally, reverse it, take another image from memory, superimpose it over the first, and print the combined picture in a matter of seconds.

I was extremely disappointed to learn that a laser printer is not, as I had hoped, a dangerous machine that uses a ray gun to burn crisp black letters on clean sheets of paper. It is, instead, a xerographic device in which the laser is used to "write" directly on the surface of the photoreceptor, which then turns out a hard copy in the manner prescribed by Chester Carlson. As has often happened over the years, Xerox was the first to think of laser printing but not the first to use it in a commercial product.

Laser xerography will play a large role in the much-discussed office of the future. A laser, in combination with a microprocessor, makes it possible to create copies without originals. Futuristic secretaries, hovering above the floor in streamlined rocket chairs, will create lavishly illustrated documents on their desktop microcomputers and transmit them instantaneously halfway around the world, where they will be printed, collated, and bound on laser copiers without the intervention of human hands.

Actually, everything except the hovering is already being done. In the future it will continue to be done, only more so. Canon builds laser printers and licenses its technology to a number of other companies, including Hewlett-Packard and Apple. Xerox has made up for its early hesitation with several laser printers of its own. As has already begun to be apparent, working in the office of the future will be a lot more fun for secretaries than for executives, who will spend more and more of their time figuring out ways to lay their hands on some of that neat stuff.

*L*ooking back from my relatively modest home office of the present, it is amusing to recall how strange and unfamiliar xerography once seemed. Shortly after the 914 was introduced, a journal for librarians pointed out, in the tone of voice that Christopher Columbus must have used to describe the coast of San Salvador to Queen Isabella, that the curious new machine might be used to make copies of old books. In a 1967 *New Yorker* profile of the Xerox Corporation, author John Brooks described an even more astonishing application:

One rather odd use of xerography insures that brides get the wedding presents they want. The prospective bride submits her list of preferred presents to a department store; the store sends the list to its bridal-registry counter, which is equipped with a Xerox copier; each friend of the bride, having been tactfully briefed in advance, comes to this counter and is issued a copy of the list, whereupon he does his shopping and then returns the copy with the purchased items checked off, so that the master list may be revised and thus ready for the next donor. ("Hymen, iö Hymen, Hymen!")

In the early days of the automobile, I suppose, it was not thought unusual to point out that the new invention might be employed to "facilitate travel," and so on. Nowadays I find it much more difficult to discover things that xerography *cannot* be used for. I now have at least two of almost everything I once had one of. My only regret is that these copies were made without the intervention of a laser. I mentioned this to a friend, who in turn showed me an article from *The New York Times* in which it was pointed out that much of the photocopying done today is entirely unnecessary.

An interesting point, I thought. I took it home and made a copy.

(1986)

IX.
THE MAN WHO INVENTED SATURDAY MORNING

----

*R*uth Cronk knows more interesting facts about Barbie than most people know about anything. For example: If Barbie were blown up to human size, her measurements would be 39–21–33. Barbie and Ken, her boyfriend, were named after the real children of Ruth Handler, Barbie's creator, the wife of one of the founders of Mattel, Inc., and the driving force behind the company for many years. When Ken was introduced in 1961, Handler wanted him to be what is referred to nowadays as "anatomically correct," but Mattel's (male) marketing department said no. When you rotated the arm of Growing Up Skipper (1975), her breasts got bigger. When you pulled apart the legs of Guardian Goddess, a sort of outer-space Barbie introduced in 1980, her arms flew up and her clothes fell off. If all the Barbies ever sold were laid end to end, they would span so many football fields that you would soon realize that more than 250 million Barbie-family dolls have been sold.

Cronk is a contagiously cheerful middle-aged housewife

from the Bronx. She is also the president of the International Barbie Doll Collectors Club, the editor and publisher of the *Barbie Gazette,* and probably the world's leading authority on the world's leading fashion doll. She is giving a lecture entitled "The Barbie Family" to about a dozen members of a doll-collecting club in the basement of Brooklyn's St. James Evangelical Lutheran Church. Hanging on the wall behind her is a banner made of green plastic fringe that says, in yellow fake-bamboo letters, "Aloha." (This is part of the church, not part of her presentation.) Spread out on the table before her are numerous Barbies, Kens, Midges, Francies, and other dolls, along with a broad sampling of their furniture, dogs, horses, automobiles, and, of course, clothes. (Mattel says that Barbie's vast wardrobe has made the company the world's largest producer of women's wear.)

Ruth Cronk owns more than three thousand Barbies. She has an original 1959 Barbie (along with the box it came in) that is worth perhaps $1,000. She has Barbies with Western features that are sold in Japan. She has Barbies with Asian features that are sold in the United States. She has Tiffs. She has Kellys. She has a discontinued black friend of Tutti's (Tutti is Barbie's tiny sister, fraternal twin of Todd) that was sold only in Germany.

Barbie was not an immediate hit when she was introduced to the toy trade twenty-seven years ago. Buyers thought, among other things, that she was too small and too busty to catch on with little girls and their staid, Ike-loving moms. Sears, Roebuck and Co. didn't order any of the dolls at all. But the ones that did make their way into stores were snapped up so fast that Mattel had trouble supplying replacements.

Since then the Barbie trade has been everything that the

toy trade in general has not. While Barbie and her family have been a sturdy, reliable success, the business of keeping children amused has been volatile. Fads have come and gone, and companies have followed. Mattel's own history reflects the whimsicality of the entire enterprise. Since its founding in 1945, the company has risen from obscurity to become the world's largest toy manufacturer, plunged to near bankruptcy, and pulled itself back together.

In the midst of all that jumping around, the industry as a whole has grown dramatically, generating $12 billion in sales in 1985, up from $7 billion in 1980. This growth has had several sources. Various demographic trends have conspired to make today's children more likely to be given more toys by more people who have more money to spend. (Notably, the increase in the number of remarriages following divorce has increased the ratio of grandparents to children, which has increased the ratio of presents to birthdays.) The flourishing of Toys R Us and other so-called toy supermarkets has helped extend the toy-selling season beyond the traditional Thanksgiving-to-Christmas crush. A boom in character licensing has made it possible for children to own their favorite characters in the form of not merely toys but also wallpaper and breakfast cereal. Perhaps most important of all, toy manufacturers have become vastly more sophisticated (some would say insidious) at marketing their products. Television in particular has become a marketing tool, with the effect that many new TV programs for children are extended commercials for toys. Major toy introductions are now minutely planned campaigns in which tens and even hundreds of millions of dollars are at stake.

Barbie and her friends haven't just been standing around

letting their arms fly up while all this upheaval has been taking place. Ken is still a goody-goody and Barbie's feet are still shaped for high-heeled shoes, but a lot of other things about them have changed. This year, for example, Barbie has acquired a brand-new glow-in-the-dark evening gown, a brand-new glow-in-the-dark (single) bed, a brand-new glow-in-the-dark vanity, and a brand-new pet tropical bird with reversible wings. She has also acquired her very own rock band, called the Rockers. ("Don't ask me to comment about their makeup," says Ruth Cronk.)

What is Barbie, the most steadfastly unhip foot-tall person in America, doing in a rock band? The answer has to do with something else Barbie acquired this year: her first serious competitor in a long time. This competitor, whose name is Jem, also has her very own rock band, called the Holograms. When Jem's manufacturer, Hasbro, Inc., invited little girls to enter a contest by dialing 1–800–ROCKGEM and singing the Jem theme song ("Jem is truly outrageous, truly, truly, truly outrageous," etc.), so many of them did that the phone company had to put in extra lines.

Nobody, including Jem's creators, thinks that Jem is going to render Barbie obsolete. But some observers think that Jem might give Barbie a fairly interesting run for some of her money. How the contest turns out will depend on the vagaries of one of the least predictable pursuits in all of capitalism: selling fun to children.

*I*n the olden days, children had no toys per se but played with pine cones and lumps of coal. This made them happier, smarter, and better behaved than today's children, and everyone, except today's children, would like for the olden days to return.

Eventually, a few rudimentary playthings came into being: Erector sets, Tinkertoys, Lionel trains, Lincoln Logs. The children of the twenties and thirties, looking like miniature black-and-white versions of their present selves, played with these primitive amusements, covered them with the interesting-smelling dust of history, and handed them down to us. I remember playing with my father's Lincoln Logs, happily building and rebuilding the same small rectangular structure, for about five minutes. Then, the Lincoln Logs became lost. (Actually, Lincoln Logs are still popular enough to consume four carloads of Ponderosa pine trees from Oregon every month. They were invented in 1916 by John Lloyd Wright, a son of the famous architect, and were inspired by a Japanese technique for building earthquake-proof buildings.)

The first great watershed in the development of toys-as-we-know-them was the end of the Second World War. The Great Depression had made it impossible for most people to buy a lot of toys. The war had the same effect. When prosperity returned and the people now known as Yuppies began to be born, the modern toy industry was born as well. Propelling it toward maturity were the two great engines of postwar American culture: television and plastic.

Today the toy business is dominated by a handful of companies, the largest five of which—Hasbro, Mattel, Coleco Industries, Kenner Parker Toys (which consists of Kenner and Parker Brothers, a venerable game manufacturer), and Fisher-Price—accounted for more than 45 percent of all toys sold in 1985. Of these five, only Fisher-Price began—in 1930—as a toy company. Kenner began in 1947 as a soap and soft-drink manufacturer; a premium called the Bubbl/Matic Gun, which came in boxes of Kenner Soap, was so well received that the company switched businesses. (One-hundred-and-three-year-old Parker Brothers has always been what it is today, primarily a manufacturer of games.) Coleco started in 1932 as the Connecticut Leather Company, a wholesale distributor of shoe-repair supplies; it became a toy company, sort of, in the early 1950s when it began selling the Official Howdy Doody Make It Yourself Bee-Nee Kit and other leathercraft items for children. The first products of Mattel—whose name consists of syllables from the names of founders Harold Matson and Elliot Handler—were picture frames and miniature furniture made of polyurethane left over from the manufacture of airplane nosecones. Hasbro started out in 1923 as Hassenfeld Brothers, purveyors of textile remnants.

*U*ntil the mid-1970s as many as 70 percent of all toys sold at retail each year were sold during the six weeks before Christmas. According to the usual pattern, wholesale buyers ordered these toys each February at the American International Toy Fair (a ten-day trade show in New York City), received them in the spring or summer, and paid for them in December, a delayed billing practice known in the business as "dating." The new toys were put on the shelves in mid-autumn. By the first of the new year, the toy year was over.

Today Christmas sales account for only about half of the year's toy business. The Toy Fair has declined slightly in importance as the selling season has lengthened; new toys are now introduced year-round. By the time this Christmas rolls around, many of the most popular toys will have been on the shelves (not to mention on the tube) for months.

The person most responsible for loosening Santa's grip on

the toy business was born in the back room of a Washington, D.C., bicycle shop in 1923. "I was a quiet, introspective child," Charles Lazarus says. His father bought broken bicycles, rebuilt them, and sold them. Young Charles learned to ride and walk on roughly the same day. "I always wondered why we didn't sell new bicycles," he says. "My father said it was because the big chain stores could sell them so much cheaper than we could."

Engraving these words on the inside of his skull somewhere, Lazarus went off to the Second World War, where he served as a cryptographer. After the war he felt too old (at twenty-four) to go to college. He took over the family store, got rid of the bicycles, and filled the place with baby furniture. It was a good business; returning soldiers were having large families. Over the course of several years, though, Lazarus noticed something interesting: People who bought one crib seldom bought another. Baby furniture didn't wear out. He began to think about merchandise that would. "Toys are a great kind of thing to sell, because they don't last that long," he says today. Lazarus switched to the toy business and named his store the Children's Supermart. To increase name recognition, he printed the R's backward.

As Lazarus expanded his business, he decided that his signs didn't look right. If two long words were to fit on a sign, the letters had to be small. Shorter words, bigger letters. He set out to find the shortest possible name that would convey what he was selling. He settled on Toys R Us, retaining a backward R.

The whole structure of retailing was under renovation in the 1950s as Lazarus was hammering out his strategy for selling toys. The age of discounting had arrived. Lazarus re-

trieved his father's pronouncement from his cranium and studied the experience of the cut-rate chain E. J. Korvette. The
key to success, Lazarus decided, was offering name-brand
merchandise at less than list price. In 1966, having opened
three additional outlets, Lazarus sold his business to a company called Interstate Stores for $7.5 million. Lazarus himself
was part of the package, staying on to manage his stores. Over
the next eight years he added forty-three new outlets.

While Toys R Us prospered, though, the rest of Interstate gradually fell apart, finally filing for bankruptcy in 1974.
The company was reorganized in 1978, under the Toys R Us
name, with Lazarus as chief executive officer. The new company's early days were difficult, but toy manufacturers extended extremely generous credit terms to keep Lazarus in
business. Toys R Us quickly entered a period of rapid growth
that made it, in the words of a recent research report from
the international banking and brokerage firm Goldman, Sachs
& Co., "one of the outstanding companies in all of retailing."
Between 1975 and 1985, the company's annual revenues grew
from a little over $200 million to a little over $2 billion.

Toy manufacturers were willing to back Lazarus because
they believed that Toys R Us was the key to what they
yearned for: year-round toy sales. Unlike traditional toy retailers, Lazarus didn't cut his stocks back dramatically in the
off-season. Nor did he pick and choose among manufacturers'
offerings; he usually ordered the entire catalogue, and he put
at least one of everything out where customers could see it.

Visiting a Toys R Us store for the first time is quite an
experience. The stores look like warehouses. Toys are stacked
nearly to the ceiling, and the customers push shopping carts.
The selection—more than eighteen thousand different toys in

every store—is almost inconceivably vast. "There's an enormous opportunity in America if you're willing to make a commitment to inventory," Lazarus says.

Like striped toothpaste, seedless grapes, and many other great ideas, the Toys R Us concept is relatively simple. The most important element is central control. Toys R Us managers never place orders; new toys simply arrive. A computerized merchandise-tracking system links every cash register in each of the 233 American Toys R Us outlets with corporate headquarters in Rochelle Park, New Jersey. If the Toys R Us in Christiana, Delaware, is running low on Immortals of Change Attack Probes, the computer notifies the nearest distribution center and Attack Probes are shipped to the store.

Decisions made at Toys R Us now affect every aspect of the toy business. Before Lazarus, dolls were kept in closed boxes, *behind* toy counters. Now toy packaging is designed with a view to how it will look (and whether it will fit) on the shelves at Toys R Us. Because Toys R Us stacks toys high into the air, virtually all packages are now made to stack.

Toys R Us has become important to the success of most toys, and manufacturers check with Rochelle Park before they go into production. "By early December," Lazarus says, "we've seen nearly everything that will be introduced at Toy Fair. In fact, we've seen more, because some goods get dropped along the way." Very often, the goods that are dropped are goods that didn't appeal to Lazarus and his staff. Some toys are even tested in the stores before a final decision is made. A company planning a new toy for Christmas of one year might make a small number of samples and ship them to Toys R Us as early as September of the year before.

Toys R Us has been so successful that the rest of the

retail toy business has had to change in order to survive. The company has attracted a number of imitators, including Child World, Lionel Leisure, and a host of regional chains. Big discount chains like K mart and Caldor used to run their toy departments the way Macy's did, expanding them for Christmas and contracting them during the rest of the year. Now the discounters and even Macy's have discovered that if they don't maintain competitive toy departments all year long, their customers defect to Toys R Us during the off-season, and don't come back for Christmas. In the meantime, traditional department stores have essentially stopped selling toys.

Toys R Us customers are very loyal. The chain has a no-questions-asked return policy that grew out of a discovery Lazarus made when he was starting out in business. "I noticed that the customer who raised his voice generally got his purchase taken back anyway, regardless of the merits," he says. Toys R Us also carries a selection of children's clothing and other non-toy merchandise—most notably disposable diapers, which the company buys by the megaton and sells at near or below cost. Many customers come to Toys R Us to stock up on Huggies and then spend the savings on toys. (The company has also found that its customers buy toys with the money they save buying other toys; people generally come to Toys R Us planning to spend a certain amount of money, not to make specific purchases.)

All in all, the strategy has been astonishingly successful. Close to 16 percent of the money Americans spend on toys is spent at Toys R Us, and analysts say the figure could eventually go as high as 40 percent, a market share unprecedented in retailing. Almost everywhere Lazarus looks, he sees trends that make him smile: parents are having fewer children and spending more money on each one; working mothers are feeling guilty about not seeing their children and making it up to them with toys; in 1990, there will be 15.1 percent more children between the ages of five and nine than there were in 1983.

Lazarus also likes what he sees overseas. There are now Toys R Us stores in Canada, the United Kingdom, and Singapore, and many more stores are planned in Europe and elsewhere. Any country that has supermarkets, Lazarus says, is a potential home for Toys R Us. That goes double for any country with commercial TV. Here at home, the company has been expanding its number of outlets at a rate of roughly 18 percent a year.

*I*n a world where people disagree about almost everything, it's reassuring that there is a single, universally accepted standard for judging toys. This standard can be stated simply: A toy is appropriate for my child if I had either it or something almost exactly like it when I was growing up.

My favorite toy when I was growing up was a smallish set of Lego building blocks. Lego is not an American toy. It is the product of Interlego A/S, a privately held multinational corporation based in Billund, Denmark. The company began in 1916 as the Billund Woodworking and Carpenter's Shop. The proprietor was a young joiner named Ole Kirk Christiansen. One of his biggest projects was rebuilding the Billund Woodworking and Carpenter's Shop, which two of his sons accidentally burned to the ground in 1924. When the Depression hit, Ole began making ironing boards and stepladders. Then to save scarce raw materials, he began making miniature ironing boards and stepladders. He sold them as toys.

The toy business was good to Ole, and soon he devoted his full attention to it. He had great success with the yo-yo, a toy that reached Denmark in the early 1930s. (It was introduced to the United States in 1929 by Donald Duncan, who also invented the parking meter.) Then, abruptly, the market for yo-yos vanished. Ole unfortunately had a warehouse full of them. Facing ruin, he was suddenly inspired: he sawed the yo-yos in half and used them as wheels on toy trucks.

In 1934, Ole offered a prize to the employee who suggested the best name for the company. The winner was Ole himself, who thought of Lego, from the Danish words *leg godt*, meaning play well. After the Second World War plastic was incorporated into the line. One of the company's first plastic toys, introduced in 1949, was a product originally called "automatic binding bricks." These were small plastic bricks that had round studs on top, enabling them to be snapped together.

In the 1950s, control of the company gradually passed to Ole's son Godtfred, usually referred to by his initials, GKC. (Today the company is run by GKC's son Kjeld Kirk Kristiansen, who changed the spelling of his last name.) In 1954, GKC took a fateful boat ride across the North Sea during the course of which he devised what are known today as "The 10 Lego Characteristics." These include: "unlimited play possibilities"; "enthusiasm to all ages"; "always topical"; "safety and quality"; "more Lego—multiplied play value"; "imagination, creativity, development." To translate somewhat, GKC decided that the ideal toy was one that both left and suggested much to the imagination, that was not limited in its appeal, and that could be expanded indefinitely, creating the possibility of multiple sales.

(GKC was certainly correct to focus on the imagination, the child's most important plaything. When I was in grade school, a classmate took an electric barber's razor and shaved some little rectangles on his head—parking spaces for his Matchbox cars. His mother was apoplectic, but the parking lot was his to keep until his hair grew back.)

Upon returning to Billund, GKC concluded that only one of the company's two-hundred-plus products satisfied all of these requirements. Thenceforward, he decreed, the company would concentrate on plastic bricks, renamed the Lego System of Play.

What GKC conceived in 1954 was the blueprint for a toy line that need never go out of style. A few wooden toys continued to be manufactured until 1960, but GKC was convinced of the soundness of his vision. The years have borne him out. Today Lego bricks are sold in 125 countries, including the Soviet Union and Israel (which boasts the highest per capita Lego sales in the world). They can be found in roughly 40 percent of American homes with children under the age of fifteen, and have the second-highest "coverage" of any toy (the first-place coverer is Crayola Crayons). In some European countries, Lego's coverage is closer to 85 percent. Some sixty-eight million children around the world spend five billion hours a year playing with Lego bricks. The company receives letters from many of these children, including this one, who wrote to Susan Williams, the fictitious head of consumer services at the company's American subsidiary in Enfield, Connecticut:

Good morning Dear FIRM "Lego" Systems!! Dear Susan!!!

My name is Morriss. I am boy! I am 10 years old. *I love "Lego."* I want to tell you thank you very so much for sending me blocks "Lego" (second-hand). I live in

Gdansk in Poland. I like very much my english lessons. I have a private lessons. My teacher of english lessons Mrs. Ola tell us about live abroad.

When I grow up I will a captain and I will send you from every one harbor a postcard to you Dear FIRM Lego and Miss Susan!

Headquarters in Billund sometimes competes with its young correspondents in innovative use of the English language. Many official proclamations are delivered in a hybrid tongue known informally within the company as Danish English, or Danglish. GKC, who speaks regular English with great hesitation, keeps the pockets of his jackets filled with little cards that have "The 10 Lego Characteristics" printed on one side and "The 10 Lego Rules" printed on the other. The Rules are sometimes reminiscent of the Characteristics: "Be positive and unpretentious"; "Be international"; "Observe characteristics"; "Take precedence of sublimate self."

When the Lego System began, the bricks were aimed primarily at five- and six-year-olds. Over the years the target audience has been extended both up and down. There are now Lego products for children as young as three months old. The upper age limit is officially given as fourteen years, but the bricks are very popular with older children and even with adults, who, when bitten, tend to buy enormous quantities. My daughter loves her Duplo blocks, outsize Lego bricks intended for preschoolers. (Some of the smaller bricks present a choking hazard for children under three.) Consistent with GKC's notion of a system of play, Duplo bricks, though eight times the volume of standard Lego bricks, can be snapped together with their smaller cousins. The innovation that makes this possible, hollow studs on the Duplo bricks, came to GKC in a dream.

In Denmark, GKC is a figure of Disneyesque proportions. His Legoland amusement park is one of the country's major tourist attractions. Almost everything at Legoland is made of Lego bricks. Popular attractions include models of Mt. Rushmore (1.5 million bricks), the space shuttle *Columbia* (410,000), Hans Christian Andersen (210,000), the Port of Copenhagen (3 million), and Egypt's Abu Simbel temples (265,000 bricks). There is also a Wild West town, called Legoredo, where the cowboys eat "twists of tenderfoot bread," speak Danish, and wear clogs. More than 14 million people have visited Legoland since it opened, in 1968.

That Lego has been as successful as it has been in the United States is a tribute more to the fundamental soundness of the toy than to the way it has been marketed here. Executives in Billund like to believe that Lego should sell simply because it's Lego, a notion that runs against the very grain of American civilization. Some toy-industry analysts tend to believe that the company could sell a lot more bricks in this country if it put its mind to it.

*I*f the Danes ever decide to take a crash course in American toy marketing, a good teacher would be Bernard Loomis. Loomis is a great big man who wears glasses and likes to play tennis. Over the years he has ascended to mythic stature in the toy business. He has worked for the largest toy company in the world, at the moment it became the largest toy company, on three separate occasions. Almost every time the industry has made a major, controversial step in the last twenty-five years, Bernie Loomis has been in the neighborhood.

Bernard Loomis was born in the Bronx in 1923. His father was a Russian immigrant who dabbled in show business and generally failed to make a living as an itinerant salesman of woolen goods. "Ours was a family whose economics were always confused," Loomis says. There was no money for toys; among young Bernard's only playthings were a Lionel train catalog, which he knew backward and forward, and a vivid imagination. One year he played a full American League baseball season using a deck of cards. He had developed an elaborate system in which every card he turned over meant something specific: a ball, a strike, a double, a pop fly. In fat notebooks he kept track not only of scores but also of pitching records and batting averages. By the time the World Series rolled around, he had played every game in the schedule.

Loomis attended New York University at night and held down a succession of dead-end jobs. "I fooled around in a lot of things in some kind of search that even I didn't understand," he says. By the late 1950s he was working in New York as a toy manufacturer's representative, having lately retired from the hardware business. At the 1961 Toy Fair he met Ruth and Elliot Handler, of Mattel (who had bought out Harold Matson and now ran the company together). He liked the Handlers and their colleagues immediately, and accepted their offer of a job.

Mattel was a small company at the time, but it was on the verge of becoming the driving force in the industry. "Much of what the toy business is today started with Mattel in the late 1950s," Loomis says. "That was when the industry changed from being a customer-driven business, where the customer decided what he wanted, to being a consumer-communication business."

In a word, television. The first step had come in 1955, before Loomis arrived, when Mattel had bought half a million dollars' worth of commercial time on the new Mickey Mouse Club show. It was, according to lore, the first time that toys— beginning with an item called a Mouse Guitar—had been advertised on national television. (The first toy advertised on local TV may have been Hasbro's Mr. Potato Head, which was pitched in California in 1952.)

Television expanded the market for new toys and made it possible for manufacturers to spend more money on new products. It also enabled retailers to cut their prices, since the increased customer traffic permitted narrower profit margins. The new way of life evolved further in 1960 with the introduction of Chatty Cathy, the world's first talking doll and a toy whose marketing strategy Loomis helped devise. Chatty Cathy could never have been produced in the days before television; the potential market would have been too small to justify the cost of developing the doll's talking mechanism. With television, the demand for Chatty Cathy was so great that some retailers began to sell it at less than cost in order to steer the crowds into their stores—a radical step in a business where merchandise had traditionally sold for double its wholesale price.

In 1969 Loomis and others at Mattel undertook what would eventually be seen as an epochal step in the marriage between toys and television. Mattel had introduced a line of miniature cars called Hot Wheels. Instead of simply advertising them on television, why not give them an entire show of their own? The thirty-minute Hot Wheels cartoon show joined

ABC's Saturday-morning lineup. The show, developed in close collaboration with Mattel, featured cars from the Hot Wheels line.

The new show didn't just catch the attention of children. It was also noticed by Topper Corporation, a now-defunct competitor of Mattel's. Topper complained to the Federal Communications Commission that *Hot Wheels* violated FCC regulations concerning the separation of programming and advertising. The FCC agreed, and asked stations to log part of the show as advertising time—a move that seemed to deter the formation of any similar alliances between broadcasters and toy companies.

Loomis and Mattel, it turned out, had merely been ten years ahead of their time. During the decade it took their time to catch up, Loomis left Mattel to become the president of Kenner Products, at the time a foundering subsidiary of General Mills. Loomis turned the company around with a string of hit toys, including a licensed "action figure" (as most dolls for boys are known) based on the television series *The Six Million Dollar Man.*

The Six Million Dollar Man doll was a big success, and Loomis began looking for other properties to license. One day in 1976, he noticed a brief item in the *Daily Hollywood Reporter* about a movie that was then being made. Loomis had never heard of the director before, but he liked the title: *Star Wars.* "I circled the item and sent a copy to a man in our marketing group, and I said, 'Find out about this.' " A short time later he and Twentieth Century-Fox Film Corporation signed an agreement giving Kenner exclusive rights to manufacture crafts, games, and toys based on the motion picture.

The agreement didn't cost Kenner very much. Toys based

on movies had seldom sold well, and outer space was thought to be a poisonous theme. But Loomis wasn't interested in the movie; all he cared about was the characters. "I contend that George Lucas is one of the world's great toy designers," he says today. Kenner's line wasn't scheduled to appear until roughly a year after *Star Wars* had been released, by which time, Loomis assumed, the movie would have been forgotten. The characters, he believed, were strong enough to stand alone.

He never had a chance to find out if he was right. From the day it opened, *Star Wars* was a phenomenal success. Children were sitting through it a dozen, two dozen times. "We had a tiger by the tail," Loomis says today. Christmas was just around the corner, and Kenner wouldn't be able to ship toys until spring; the *Star Wars* line had been planned for the *following* Christmas. The toys were being manufactured overseas, and there was no way to speed up production. Could anything be done?

Loomis pondered the problem for a long time, then had an idea: why not sell the toys before they existed? Kenner could print a certificate promising to deliver toys by a certain date and package it with a picture of the *Star Wars* characters. Parents would have something to put under the Christmas tree, and kids could at least hang the picture in their rooms until spring. Loomis called a meeting of his staff and presented the idea. They all thought it was crazy.

Loomis was taken aback. "But I believed that one of my duties as head of a toy company was to lose at least a million dollars a year on things that didn't happen," he says. "So I went ahead." The promotion turned out to be a huge success. Children were happy to receive the pictures. When their toys finally arrived by mail, they took them to school and sent jealous friends rushing to toy stores. *Star Wars* eventually generated more than $750 million dollars in toy sales.

Star Wars confirmed what *The Six Million Dollar Man* had first shown, which was that licensed characters could be the basis for very lucrative toys. But *Star Wars* also showed that the logistics of producing such toys could be complicated: there were many factors beyond the toy company's control. If only it were somehow possible to manage the entire package from beginning to end.

By 1978, Loomis had become head of General Mills' Toy Group (which included Kenner and Parker Brothers). One day he met with representatives of American Greetings Corporation, a publisher of greeting cards. American Greetings owned the licensing rights to a popular cartoon character called Ziggy and wondered whether Loomis might be interested in producing a Ziggy toy.

Loomis said no. Ziggy was already established in the marketplace. There were greeting cards, a syndicated comic strip, and other tie-ins. Loomis wasn't interested in simply tagging along. "But I told them, sort of casually, 'If you ever have a project where you want a partner from day one, come back and see me again.' " As it happened, the men had a copy of American Greetings' catalog for the following year. Loomis flipped through the pages, then stopped. There was a character on one greeting card that looked promising. Loomis pointed to the picture and said, "Mark the time and date. We're going to make history."

Actually, there are several versions of this story. In another one, Jack Chojnacki, who was the director of licensing for American Greetings, discovered that a common element in a lot of successful greeting cards and other products was strawberries. An art director heard this and remembered that one of American Greetings' most successful cards featured a little girl with strawberries on her bonnet. He had an artist add more strawberries. Then a doll was made. Chojnacki and Ralph Shaffer, the director of new-product development, took the card and the doll to Loomis, who looked at them and said, "This is going to be the next major phenomenon in merchandising."

All versions of the story have the same ending: the little girl in the greeting card became a bustling industry called Strawberry Shortcake. What was remarkable was not the character—just a little girl with berries on her clothes—but the marketing plan that was built around it. Loomis had been thinking about the uncertainties of the toy business and had decided that the way to protect against them was to concentrate on lines of toys rather than on individual products. An important reason that Barbie was successful year after year, he believed, was that Mattel had made the doll part of an imaginary environment that, with careful management, could be extended indefinitely. The key was giving the customer a reason to keep buying.

What Loomis had discovered was, in a sense, the ten Lego Characteristics. Like GKC, he believed that the secret of producing a successful toy lay in finding a concept broad enough for more than a single season. Such concepts tend to be simple: plastic building blocks, a dress-up doll, stick-on faces for vegetables. Of course, Lego, Barbie, and Mr. Potato Head (now thirty-five years old) were created through inspiration and luck, not the application of a formula. But the formula could be a useful guide in the development and marketing of humbler toys. Every toy a company produced, Loomis believed, could be a line; indeed, it should be.

For Strawberry Shortcake Loomis envisioned just such a line, with lots of characters and a story tying them together. (Strawberry Shortcake's friends have names like Lime Chiffon and Raspberry Tart; they live in Strawberryland and join together to combat a limited form of evil that manifests itself in things like disappointing fruit crops.) Loomis also wanted to involve the entire Toy Group. The girl on the greeting card would be translated into toys, games, television shows, and hundreds of licensed products, and everything would be created from scratch and centrally controlled. Loomis's idea about the importance of lines would quickly become the conventional wisdom of the industry.

*T*he first Strawberry Shortcake television special, which aired in 1980, revived a potent controversy that many people believed had been laid to rest. *Welcome to the World of Strawberry Shortcake* was clearly as much a program-length commercial as the old *Hot Wheels* cartoon show had been. But the regulatory mood in Washington had changed, and the Strawberry Shortcake special opened the way for what sometimes appears to be the transformation of children's television into a promotional arm of the toy industry.

There are now about twenty toy-based television shows. A recent Saturday-morning lineup included shows based on GoBots, Wuzzles, Snorks, M.A.S.K., Popples, and others. The shows are typically financed directly by toy companies or their licensing partners, who also control the scripts. In 1985 the FCC in effect gave its blessing to the new shows by refusing to hold hearings on product-based TV for children.

Shortly after the FCC decision, Peggy Charren, president of a consumer group called Action for Children's Television (ACT), told *Newsweek*, "We think the FCC has now completely disowned the nation's children." Charren, whose name is almost invariably preceded in print by adjectives like *indefatigable*, has been fighting broadcasters, programming producers, breakfast-cereal manufacturers, toy companies, and others on a number of issues since the late 1960s. Her organization has been instrumental in bringing about a number of changes in children's television, including a reduction in the number of minutes devoted to advertising in programs aimed at kids.

ACT's main argument against the toy-based shows is that young children draw no distinction between commercial and editorial content and are thus easy targets for manipulative marketing. Toys based on popular movie and television characters have been around for years (for example, Mickey Mouse dolls); but in the past, ACT has said, the movies and programs always came first. Now the toys often precede the programs, whose scripts are conceived as promotional tools. Furthermore, according to ACT, the toy-based shows have prevented better programming from reaching the air.

ACT has proposed a number of remedies over the years, including the banning of toy advertising from children's television and the banning of *all* advertising from children's television. More recently, as the prospects for new regulation have dimmed, ACT has retreated to a much tamer demand—that toy-based television shows be sprinkled with announcements reminding children that they are being pitched.

The toy companies more or less concede that their new programs are commercials; boastful sales pitches to retailers describe the shows in almost the same terms Peggy Charren does. When criticized, though, the toy companies also say that being on TV doesn't guarantee success for a toy; three of the most popular children's shows at the moment are the three segments of the ninety-minute cartoon show *Smurfs*, yet Smurfs toys don't sell well. Toy companies also say that toys are such a big part of the lives of children that there isn't all that much else to make shows about. Furthermore, they say, the question of which comes first, the toy or the show, is irrelevant.

There are many, many other arguments and counterarguments. The ones just cited sketch the general outline of the debate. In that debate right-thinking people tend to come down fairly quickly on the side of ACT; who can help but be appalled by all that crass commercialism? But the real issues are not as simple as Charren and her supporters make them out to be.

First of all, ACT's proposed reforms seem naive. Banning advertising from children's shows has a certain surface appeal (everybody hates commercials), but the idea is unrealistic. Why not also require toy companies to give their products away? Removing all the money from children's television would not prompt producers to create better shows. ACT's latest proposal—that toy-based shows be required to contain disclaimers identifying them as promotions—seems potentially counterproductive. If young viewers really can't distinguish between shows and commercials, then the toy companies could probably *increase* sales by reminding kids that the toys they're watching can also be bought.

Another possibility might be to prohibit toy companies from creating television programs. But how do you banish Strawberry Shortcake and Care Bears without also banishing Muppets? The Muppets' creator, Henson Associates, is on almost everyone's (including Peggy Charren's) list of top-quality producers, but the Muppets support a profitable stable of more than five hundred licensed products, many of them toys. Henson even has its own New York toy store, called Muppet Stuff. Henson Associates, whatever else it is, is an extremely successful toy business, and Henson's shows, whatever else they are, are program-length commercials. Children's Television Workshop, home of the widely acclaimed series *Sesame Street*, earns back two thirds of the show's production costs from the licensing of toys and other products.

Nor is it possible to make meaningful distinctions according to whether the toys or the shows were thought of first. To young viewers, Mickey Mouse and Strawberry Shortcake are contemporaries. What's more, there's no consistent pattern to the order in which toys and shows appear. Companies now often find it profitable to introduce toy-based shows well in advance of the toys on which they are based; "quality" producers often work out toy-licensing deals well before their new shows reach the air. Hairsplitting examinations of the "intentions" of the programming producers lead nowhere.

The real question has to do not with toy companies but with the quality of children's television, which is abysmal. Sitting through a full Saturday or Sunday morning of kidvid, as I dutifully did several times in the course of researching this essay, is a pretty horrifying experience. "Speaking of Girza, it's time to move on to Bandasar and take care of Tormac," and so on and so on, hour after hour. Much of ACT's support, I suspect, comes from people who feel the same way: the kids' shows are horrible; let's do something about the people who make them.

But program quality is a quicksand subject for people who, like Peggy Charren, believe in the First Amendment. In its most recent petition to the FCC, ACT stresses that it "does not seek to ban or impede the presentation" of the toy-based shows but merely to make explicit to young viewers the programs' commercial intent. ACT has also been quick to condemn various right-wing groups that periodically call for the elimination of television shows they find offensive. To confront directly what is genuinely bothersome about children's television—its mindlessness—is to come uncomfortably close to advocating censorship.

ACT addresses the quality issue only obliquely, by claiming that having to satisfy the requirements of toy manufacturers stifles the creativity of the people who put shows together, and that children's programming would improve if the toy companies cleared out. In an article in *PTA Today* in 1985, ACT's director of development quoted a television producer as saying, "I would love to create shows rather than have someone come in and say, 'This is the golden ashtray everyone's buying; give me a show about it.' " Charren has said, "It's a shame we don't have diversity of producers for children's TV. Certainly they'd like to be there, but it's the money powers that are playing the ratings game who keep them out."

"Money powers" and "ratings game" are buzz phrases calculated to heat the blood of caring persons, but unless one rejects the idea of commercial TV, there's nothing sinister about the people they signify (respectively, advertisers and viewers). In fact, commercial television is one of the few truly democratic institutions around: We "vote" by watching, and the shows we don't watch don't stay on the air. Charren has said the networks could field better programs if they wanted to, because "broadcasters know what good programming is. Those are the ones they submit for awards." This is a specious argument. Book publishers must know what good books are (the ones they submit for awards); why don't they print more of them?

The solution to the kidvid program—the real kidvid problem—is simple: If the shows weren't watched, they wouldn't be on. Parents complain about the quality of the shows but don't prevent their children from gluing themselves to the boob tube. In the end, the garbage on TV is probably a fairly accurate representation of what the audience (parents included) really wants. There was a vast outpouring of public protest when CBS canceled *Captain Kangaroo*, in 1981, but the show's ratings had been microscopic for years. No one wanted to see it go, but no one wanted to see it, either.

The well-known discrepancy between what parents say and what they do arises in this case from a deep ambivalence about television. On the one hand, almost everyone at least pays lip service to the idea that watching a lot of TV is bad; on the other hand, television has become a sort of national babysitting service. According to the A. C. Nielsen Company's 1986 Report on Television, children between the ages of two and five watch an average of twenty-eight hours and fifteen minutes of television a week. Their most active viewing period is weekdays between ten in the morning and four-thirty in the afternoon. Busy parents (or the sitters they hire) are using television to keep their children quiet. This is a great tragedy. But the responsibility for it belongs to parents.

Most of the toy-based shows are crummy, but so are most of the other shows. *Scooby Doo*, a cartoon show created before the toy companies invaded Saturday morning, is not a better program than *Snorks*. *Sesame Street* is reflexively admired by almost everyone, but adults would praise it less if they watched it more. *Sesame Street* may not be total schlock, but kids often watch it the way they watch total schlock: like zombies. Four hours of television a day is much too much, even if it's Bert and Ernie. ACT for years has paradoxically called upon the networks to provide *more* television shows aimed at children during *more* hours of the week. Kids might be better off if broadcasters got rid of children's shows and filled kids' favorite time slots with the one kind of programming most of them can't stand: news.

To fail to be appalled by the connection between toy companies and children's television is not to endorse the shows. But it is possible to find a few nice things to say about them. First, toy-based programs at least encourage children to spend some of their waking hours away from the television set: a child who wheedles his parents into buying him a toy he's seen on TV will presumably play with it once in a while. Second, the new shows have a number of features missing from a lot of other shows—particularly widely admired cartoon "classics" like *Popeye* and *Tom and Jerry*—such as racial balance, uplifting sentiments, and, for the most part, a conspicuous lack of violence. Third, the substantial cost of creating television shows has encouraged toy companies to favor products that are well thought out, well designed, and not likely to disappear overnight: fad toys don't earn back multimillion-dollar television investments. Fourth . . .

Well, three is pretty many.

*I*f Bernie Loomis helped invent the strategy of concentrating on expandable lines of toys, Hasbro has come close to perfecting it. In an industry where violent, unruly expansion and retraction is the rule, Hasbro's rise to preeminence in the industry has been impressive. The company has lately become a darling of the nation's financial analysts and business magazines, which have praised it for unusually sound management.

Most observers give credit for Hasbro's success to the company's young chairman, Stephen Hassenfeld. Hassenfeld, forty-four, and his brother, Alan, thirty-seven, who is Hasbro's president, represents their family's third generation in the toy business. Unlike Charles Lazarus and Bernard Loomis, Stephen and his brother had lots and lots of toys when they were growing up. Their father, Merrill, was widely admired in the industry, and executives of other companies often showed their affection by showering his sons with gifts. The head of the company that manufactured Lionel trains even added young Stephen's name to his list of salesmen, which meant that every time a new train or accessory came out, Stephen received a sample. Directing one of the world's most spectacular train sets around his basement, he knew from a very early age what he wanted to do when he grew up.

Over the last ten years or so, Stephen has to a large extent succeeded in making Hasbro what all toy companies yearn to be: a rational enterprise. Selling toys has always been a fashion business. Companies have scored inebriating successes alongside sobering failures, all subject to the largely unpredictable whims of children. The goal, seldom achieved, has been to minimize the failures without killing off the creativity that produces successes.

Hasbro's strategy for growth without trauma has focused on diversification within the toy industry. It has done this partly by acquiring other companies (most significantly, it bought Milton Bradley and its Playskool subsidiary, in 1984, for $350 million) and partly by expanding steadily into new toy categories. This strategy is now nearly universal, or universally aspired to, in the industry. Tonka Corporation, formerly known only as an unflashy manufacturer of high-quality toy trucks, now offers a greatly expanded selection that also includes GoBots, a Cabbage Patch-inspired line of stuffed dogs called Pound Puppies, and Rock Lords, transformable figures described on their cartoon show as "powerful living rocks." Tonka's expansion has been very successful. As of 1985, the company was the sixth-largest toy manufacturer in the country.

Stephen Hassenfeld's first big hit was the 1982 reintroduction of G.I. Joe. Originally marketed as a Second World War-era infantryman in 1964, G.I. Joe was turned into a line of quasi-military "adventurers" in 1970. In succeeding years the line was expanded to include a kung fu fighter, a bionic warrior, a superhuman, and a spaceman. The line was discontinued altogether in 1978, when it was done in by a combination of high oil prices—which made its large plastic body and accessories expensive to manufacture—and a proliferation of smaller, less expensive action figures. When G.I. Joe resurfaced four years later, it had shrunk (from just under a foot to just under four inches, a size made popular by *Star Wars* toys), changed its slogan (from "a fighting man from head to toe" to "a real American hero"), and multiplied itself into a "strike force" consisting sixteen separate characters (one of which was female and none of which was actually called G.I. Joe).

The redesigned toy did $49 million in business in 1982, making it the nation's best-selling toy in the second half of the year. When Hassenfeld saw those sales figures, his first reaction was one of joy; his second was one of concern. Forty-nine million dollars represented nearly 36 percent of Hasbro's revenue at the time, making the company dangerously vulnerable to a drop in the toy's popularity. Perhaps the most important lesson Hassenfeld had learned during his lifelong tutelage in the toy business was that profit often goeth before a fall. The mistake other toymakers had habitually made, he felt, was in believing that they were immune from the tendency of booms to go bust.

This is not to say that Hassenfeld abandoned his popular new toy. Quite the contrary. But he made plans for the future of the company that didn't depend on G.I. Joe's continued success. Profits from the toy's first year were reinvested in the company's future, primarily as part of the package that financed the Milton Bradley acquisition.

*P*arents and others sometimes complain about the prevalence of lines, and the emphasis on repeated purchases, in the toy business today. Yet the modern way has much to recommend it. Nothing looks more forlorn to the person who bought it than a toy that is used a time or two and then forgotten. For a toy line to remain viable year after year, children have to continue playing with it. When line extensions predominate at Toy Fair, it means the playroom is safe for another year. Nobody throws away Lego. The emphasis on lines can help keep prices down, by giving manufacturers longer to earn back their investments. It also helps keep quality up. A line doesn't last simply because it's a line. Children go back for more only if the central concept appeals to them in some enduring way.

Enduring appeal is an idea that covers a lot of territory, of course. Strawberry Shortcake has seen better days. Barbie, by contrast, is having her biggest year ever, after more than a quarter century on the shelf. Toy analysts wonder whether her new competitor, Jem, will have anything like that staying power.

Hasbro discovered Jem, or rather ur-Jem, several years ago, when an independent toy designer showed them a male rock-star doll. The doll looked promising, and Hasbro took an option on the rights.

MTV, the rock-music television channel, had grown enormously popular. MTV is aimed primarily at teenagers and young adults, but Hasbro knew that a lot of younger kids were watching it as well. Rock videos had introduced little girls to a whole new way of thinking about fashion; eight-year-olds were asking their moms if they could dye their hair pink and cut holes in their sweatshirts and do a lot of other things that Barbie didn't do. It occurred to people at Hasbro that there might be a market for a fashion doll that looked less like Barbie and more like the people on MTV.

The Hasbro executive most responsible for keeping the project going was Maurene Souza, the vice president of marketing for girls' toys. One of the first things Souza did was work out a "back story" for the new doll. When my wife was growing up, she had a favorite doll she called Leprosy, the most beautiful-sounding word she had encountered up to that point. Nowadays dolls come not only with ready-made names but also with full-blown biographies. In time the optioned male rock star became Jem/Jerrica, "a woman with a mysterious dual identity," to quote from Hasbro's publicity:

> She's Jerrica Benton, a savvy Eighties career woman, co-owner of Star Light Music Company and benefactor of Starlight House, a shelter for homeless girls. But, with the magic of "Synergy," a super-holographic computer that filters power through her Jem Star earrings, Jerrica becomes Jem, a truly outrageous rock singing sensation.
>
> With the help of little sister Kimber and friends Aja and Shana, the four become "Jem and the Holograms," the hottest girl group since the Supremes. Exciting adventures unfold as Jerrica competes for control of Starlight [sic] Music against evil co-owner Eric Raymond, while Jem and the Holograms come up against the mischievous "bad-girl" rock band, "The Misfits."

There's also Rio, Jerrica's boyfriend, who, unlike Barbie's Ken, has a snappy wardrobe ("the *Miami Vice* look") and combable hair.

"Changing from Jem to Jerrica gives the toy a great deal of depth," says Souza. "There are clothes for being Jem; there are clothes for being Jerrica. There are things Jerrica can do; there are things Jem can do. Barbie has really been locked into the mainstream American lifestyle. Jerrica is part of that too, although she's more a woman of the world. Jem becomes the fantasy. It gives us a lot of places to go with both of them." "Synergy" is Jem's key to longevity. If MTV suddenly goes out of style, the holographic computer could change Jerrica into something else: Jem, attorney-at-law.

To spread the word about Jem, Hasbro began including ten-minute Jem segments in its syndicated Sunday morning cartoon show, *Super Sunday.* The segments were so successful that Jem was spun out into her own regular series. Each show contains original songs presented in the form of "videos."

Mattel's response was immediate. Before Toy Fair, and long before Jem's debut on *Super Sunday*, Hasbro had begun to run teaser ads of the "Jem—Coming Soon" variety in the trade press. Not long after, Mattel introduced Barbie and the Rockers (featuring Dee Dee, Dana, Diva, and Derek) and prepared to slug it out. Hasbro had been expecting a rock band, but they hadn't been expecting Barbie to be a member. Truly outrageous! Mattel has always rejected the idea of a cartoon series for Barbie, whose principal strength is that she is Everygirl, but who knows?

Hasbro's hopes for Jem are fairly modest. "We want a piece," says Souza. "There's no way we're going to put Barbie out of business."

I can't make up my mind about Jem. She's a bit taller than Barbie (they can't wear each other's clothes), and she's significantly smaller in the bosom. Rio is more appealing than Ken, who has molded plastic hair and what looks like a thyroid problem. Jem has a radio in her Rockin' Roadster, but Barbie has a shower. Hmmmm.

Then again, it isn't up to me, is it?

(1986)

X.
WORK MARRIAGE

I don't work in an office, so I miss out on a lot of things that people who do don't, such as a new pen whenever I want one, coffee breaks, comical stories about my dumb boss, the concept of the weekend, lunchtime Jazzercise with my co-workers, a mysteriously burgeoning colony of Sweet 'N Low packets in my desk, nice clothes for daytime wear, and work marriage.

Work marriage is a relationship that exists between certain people of the opposite sex who work at the same place. For example, let's suppose that you, like me, are a man. In that case your work wife would be the woman in your office who:

(a) as you walk past her desk on your way to a big meeting, tells you that you have dried shaving cream behind your ear;

(b) has lunch with you pretty often;

(c) returns stuff she borrows from your desk;

(d) tells you things about her other (home) husband that he wouldn't want you to know;

(e) waits for you to finish up so you can go down in the elevator together;

(f) complains to you without embarrassment about an uncomfortable undergarment;

(g) expects you to tell her the truth, more or less, about the thing she has done to her hair;

(h) thinks you eat, drink, and smoke exactly the right amount;

(i) knows at least one thing about you—such as the fact that you can do a pretty good imitation of Liza Minnelli—that your home wife doesn't know.

Work marriage is, in some ways, better than home marriage. For example, your work wife would never ask you why you don't just put your dishes into the dishwasher instead of leaving them in the sink—she doesn't know you do it! Also, she would never get your car wedged between two other cars in the parking lot at Bradlees, sign you up to be the pie auctioneer at a church bazaar, or grab hold of your stomach and ask, "What's this? Blubber?" She knows you only as you appear between nine and five: recently bathed, fully dressed, largely awake, and in control of your life.

My wife and I both work at home. In that sense, my home wife is also my work wife. And yet this cannot be. Our argument about whether rapidly changing channels hurts the TV does not disappear at nine o'clock on Monday morning. Like many other self-employed (and thus work-single) people, I am forced to content myself with fleeting and ultimately unsatisfying pseudo work marriages, such as my relationship with a check-out girl at the grocery store. She has a pretty good idea of what I like to eat, and I help her out sometimes by doing my own bagging, but that is about as far as it goes.

(Perhaps I have merely discovered a new, less committed type of relationship: store dating.)

The only way to have a real work marriage is, sadly, to work. Sure, I'd like a work wife someday—*someday*. But I'm not willing, right now, to get a regular job in order to have one. There are just too many things about offices (no dogs or children, no nap whenever you want one, parking problems) that rub me the wrong way.

Meanwhile, my home wife and I keep trying to work out our differences. There are some indications that we are making progress. The other day she borrowed the ruler-alarm-clock-thermometer that I used to hold down the pile of papers on my desk. This morning, without any hint from me, she brought it back. Next week maybe I'll return her scissors.

(1987)

XI.
THE DREAM OF
FINANCIAL FREEDOM

W e know statistically that the average individual in the
United States of America will achieve only one third of what
he or she is capable of achieving. One third! Also, of all the
individuals in the United States of America who are involved
in a business relationship, only 2 percent are self-starters.
This is from the latest Ohio State survey.

Okay, that's scary enough, but it gets worse: Twenty-
three percent of individuals in the United States of America
don't know what they want. Bigger house? More kids? Better
reception? They don't have a clue. They might really want a
new car but instead they add a breakfast nook to their kitchen.
Sixty-seven percent do know what they want but don't know
how to get it, which, in a lot of ways, is scarier.

That leaves just 10 percent. These are the individuals who
know what they want *and* how to get it. (We know who we're
talking about now, don't we?) Thirty percent of these very
special individuals get exactly what they want 90 percent of
the time. In addition, they are able to help other individuals
figure out what they want and how to get it. Why? Because

the speed of the leader is the speed of the group. Also because 20 percent of the people in any business organization do 80 percent of the work.

I learned all this at Crossroads to Networking, the Multilevel Marketing Executive Symposium, which was held in Salt Lake City not long ago. Salt Lake City is perhaps not the first place in the United States of America where the average individual would think of holding an executive symposium: It has no bars as we know them. You can buy a two-week membership at a private club for five dollars and then buy cocktails poured from little airline-type bottles, but you can't go into your hotel's restaurant and order a drink before dinner. Instead, generally, you have to order a bottle of non-alcoholic sparkling wine, a beverage that makes you realize fairly quickly that probably 67 percent of the reason why 90 percent of the individuals who drink wine drink wine is alcohol.

But there were some good reasons for holding Crossroads to Networking in Salt Lake City anyway. First, most people are pretty interested in seeing for themselves how much the Great Salt Lake has expanded in recent years. (A lot!) Second, Utah is an important state in multilevel marketing, usually referred to simply as MLM. This is the industry that consists of Amway, Shaklee, Mary Kay Cosmetics, Herbalife International, and other companies that market their products not through stores but through networks of salespeople. Most of these salespeople, who are usually referred to by their companies as distributors, are ordinary individuals who work out of their homes in the United States of America. They not only sell products but also recruit other individuals to be distributors. They then

earn commissions both on their own sales and on those of
the distributors they've recruited. They also earn commissions on the sales of distributors recruited by the distributors they've recruited, and on the sales of distributors
recruited by them.

The MLM industry is fairly big, according to some other
statistics I heard at Crossroads to Networking. Ten percent
of American households include at least one individual involved in MLM. Fully 80 percent of all households have been
approached by at least one MLM distributor; 40 percent have
bought something. MLM products tend to be things like health
food, diet aids, water purifiers, soap, detergent, and cosmetics. Also, increasingly, they include services. Last year Amway distributors signed up a million new customers for MCI,
the discount long-distance telephone company.

The MLM industry has taken some hard shots over
the years from the crowd that engineered the American
defeat in Vietnam, drove Nixon from the White House,
and cooked up the Iran-contra affair—that is, the media.
The media sometimes have trouble distinguishing between
MLM companies and illegal pyramid schemes. They also
tend to dwell on stories involving state investigations of
MLM companies, or assertions by government agencies
that certain MLM products don't do what their distributors
claim they do, such as grow hair, cure cancer, or reverse
the aging process.

In fairness to the media it should be said that MLM companies have often made it difficult for the media to emphasize
anything but the negative. MLM companies have a very high
failure rate; people in the industry estimate that between 90
percent and 95 percent of all MLM companies go out of busi-

ness within a year of their founding. The true rate of failure may be even higher. In addition, MLM companies tend to do most of their business with some of the more vulnerable segments of the consuming population: senior citizens, people from rural areas, people without much education, and people from California (a state that all by itself accounts for something like 20 percent of MLM purchases). MLM companies also have a history of making grandiose claims about the rapidity with which their distributors can expect to become multimillionaires.

Still, there are some good things that can be said about MLM. I don't want to risk my standing in the media by saying these things myself. Instead, I'll quote D. Jack Smith, Jr., a Harvard-trained lawyer whose Memphis law firm (which is called The Law Firm of D. Jack Smith, Jr.) represents many MLM companies. At a seminar at Crossroads to Networking Smith said, "I think that one of the great things about this industry is that—and I've said it before—I think it's one of the last frontiers. This industry has something known as ease of entry, where the little guy gets to play. It doesn't take a lot of money to start an MLM company by comparison with what it would take to buy one McDonald's franchise. I have seen companies go national that started with $5,000 in borrowed capital."

Smith might also have said (and indeed he may have said before) that MLM gives ordinary people a chance to test their mettle in the marketplace, to see where they stand in the eyes of the Almighty, and to take a stab at achieving what virtually every individual in the United States of America, whether secretly or openly, dreams of achieving: financial freedom.

When I was fourteen, I spent a few days at a big hotel in Chicago with my mother, my sister, and my brother. I don't remember the name of the hotel, but I do remember that there was a couch in the lobby where I hid cigarettes. A couple of times a day I would retrieve a pack from under one of the cushions, go into the coffee shop, and smoke about eight Marlboros in a row while I drank a Coke. When I finished the Coke, I'd swish a piece of ice around in my mouth so that my mother wouldn't know I'd been smoking.

During one of my cigarette breaks, a man sitting on the stool next to mine struck up a conversation. He said I looked like an intelligent fellow and asked me if I'd like to achieve financial freedom. I said, uh, sure. In that case, he said, I ought to come with him later to a meeting in the ballroom. I went. It was a recruitment meeting for an MLM company called Holiday Magic. The man was a distributor for the company, which sold cosmetics and other products. He said he could tell just by talking to me that I'd make a good distributor, too. I confessed that, despite the cigarettes and everything, I wasn't as old as he probably assumed. He said that didn't matter; my mother could drive me around to deliver my products.

I don't remember much of what went on at the meeting, but all MLM recruitment meetings are basically alike. Undoubtedly there was a rousing speech by a man wearing powerful after-shave and perhaps two pounds of gold jewelry. The speech would have concerned how God or his wife had finally given him the courage to abandon his dead-end job as an executive of a Fortune 500 corporation and achieve financial freedom by becoming a Holiday Magic distributor. Now he had everything he'd ever desired: company car, beautiful wife, plenty of French food, vacations whenever he wanted them. Nothing would make him happier than for us—me—to have those things, too. It wouldn't be easy; I'd have to reach down deep within myself, conquer my fear of big success, and awaken my slumbering potential for greatness. But it wouldn't be hard, either; all I'd have to do was sign up a lot of other people to do what I was doing. Every month I would earn commissions based on how hard those other people worked. Then I could start shopping around for a bank with a big enough vault to handle my deposits.

I became quite excited at that meeting but (for various hormonal reasons) never followed through on Holiday Magic, thus passing up my chance to become the richest kid in the history of eighth grade. It's probably just as well. In 1973 the Securities and Exchange Commission filed a civil complaint accusing Holiday Magic of defrauding its distributors and customers of $250 million. The following year a federal judge permanently enjoined the company from operating its pyramid marketing scheme.

As I strolled among the exhibits at Crossroads to Networking, something of that old Holiday Magic magic came back to me. The room was filled with financial opportunities. At a wooden kiosk with television monitors mounted in it, I watched a videotaped presentation for a company called Nanci Corporation International. (The kiosk belonged not to Nanci but to the company that had made the video, Mountainland Video Productions. One of Mountainland's producers is named Kelly Thayer; his wife is named Kellie Thayer.) It was a little hard to hear the Nanci soundtrack over the noise in the room, but the story was easy to follow. It involved a young boy who was always losing races and a mom who was terribly disappointed in him. Scenes of the boy losing races alternated with scenes of the mom hanging her head in shame. There were also scenes of the mom feeding the boy junk food. This went on for quite a while. The mom never seemed to see the connection between the junk food and the lost races.

Then, through a friend, the mom discovered Luv-it, a specially formulated powdered food-replacement beverage mix that looks something like Carnation Instant Breakfast. Luv-it comes in different formulations for children, grownups, and old people. It can be used in combination with either Lose-it or Gain-it, depending on whether you're too tubby or too thin.

The Nanci video also contained quite a lot of footage of Nanci herself, a really attractive woman who exercises in a leotard and has a big house, a nice family, an assistant of some kind, and a snappy red Mercedes-Benz. Nanci invented Luv-it because she wanted to give people a simple, delicious way to drink wholesome meals. Now she enjoys fabulous wealth. And the little boy? He switched from french fries to Luv-it and became a winner. His mom became a winner too; now she's a Nanci distributor.

Not far from the Mountainland Video kiosk was the booth of a company called Garden State Nutritionals. Garden State makes vitamin tablets and other health products. It sells most of them through its own retail stores. It sells others to a number of private-label distributors, including several MLM companies. Most of Garden State's exhibit had been lost in transit from New Jersey, but there were still a lot of products on display: Charcoal Caps, Chocolate Thunder ("Instant Energy Fitness Formula for Active People"), Formula AR-19, Back-Eze ("Special supplement containing Nutritional Elements

found in healthy spines and discs"), Memoraid Tablets,
Thermo Slim, Grapefruit Diet 100, Night Trim ("Extra
strength overnight reducer"—take four on an empty stomach
before bed), Snooze 'N Lose. Overnight reducers are supposed
to activate your growth-hormone releasers, so that you lose
weight while you sleep.

Would activating your growth-hormone releasers make
you get old sooner? I don't know; I'm not a doctor. To be safe,
you might also want to take some CoQ_{10}, sometimes known
as the youth pill. CoQ_{10} was on display at the AlphaPak booth,
across the way from Garden State. It's an essential dietary
coenzyme nutrient that scavenges free radicals, promotes cellular energy conversion, deters oxidation, and offsets CoQ_{10}
deficiency caused by aging, according to a sign on the table.
Oxidation, another exhibitor told me, is the cause of most
disease. CoQ_{10} is made from fermented potatoes; it can also
be extracted from the hearts of cows but (fortunately) this is
too expensive to do.

I wandered around for a while trying to produce enough
saliva in my mouth to get rid of the taste of a milk substitute
called Tofu White (warm water with baby powder in it?) that
I had been persuaded to drink at the Great American Foods
booth. At another booth I drank some aloe-and-cranberry
juice, which didn't so much solve the tofu problem as make it
more complicated. I ended up sucking on the insides of my
cheeks in front of the booth of a company called Health Flo.
"Beecome a Beeliever," said a sign on the booth; "Add Health
Flo pure bee pollen products to your company," said another.
Earlier I had spoken with a woman from a company that sold
Swedish flower pollen. I asked a man at the Health Flo booth
whether Swedish flower pollen was the same thing as bee
pollen. He said it was not.

"The basic difference," he said, "is that bee pollen is collected by bees, while the other people collect their pollen with a machine. We've tested it, and bees are more discriminating. Different pollens are more desirable than others. If you put them out there, the bees will go to the more desirable one. Plus, the bees have been doing it for millions of years. The other thing that sets us apart from being just another bee pollen company is that we've developed a process for putting together a pure-bee-pollen tablet without fillers or binders. We've also been able to liquefy and stabilize— the key word being stabilize—pure bee pollen. As far as we know, we're the only company in the free world that's been able to do that."

While he was talking, a woman working with him took a bee pollen tablet from one of the bottles on the table and chewed it up. (Her commitment to bee-oriented health may not be all it appeared to be, though; later I saw her drinking a Pepsi.) When the man was finished, the woman gave me a packet of bee-pollen pills, a packet of propolis pills, and some literature. The literature described bee pollen as "the only food in the world with all the essential ingredients necessary to sustain life." It referred to propolis as an "antibiotic" whose apparently recent rediscovery "may well be one day as important as the development of penicillin." (Propolis is stuff that bees make to "keep their hive in a more sterile, hygenic [sic] condition than even a modern day operating room").

Ordinarily I have a pretty high resistance to doing anything that is supposed to be good for me, even if it doesn't sound nutty. But a week later, when I was back at home, I got sort of interested in my packets of pollen and propolis pills. One of Health Flo's brochures quoted a Dr. Sigmund Schmidt, a cancer specialist from "Germany," as saying that bee pollen "could be a cancer-preventative." Other experts were quoted as saying that pollen can reverse aging of the skin and relieve allergies, fatigue, colds, weakness, asthma, bronchitis, ulcers, colitis, migraine headaches, urinary disorders, enumeresis, multiple sclerosis, and wrinkling. What the heck! I took one bee pollen pill and one propolis pill.

A couple of hours later, while I was out working in my yard—and I'm not saying that this discredits the entire industry—I was stung by a bee.

As interesting as they are, MLM products don't tell the whole MLM story. In fact, they don't tell much of the story at all. In many companies, the products are an afterthought. The real meat of an MLM company—the thing that gets distributors excited—is usually the compensation plan.

There are many different names for MLM compensation plans: stairstep, breakaway, matrix, several others. All such plans differ one from another, but all are alike in that they derive from that most magical of mathematical phenomena, exponential growth. The Sunrider Corporation—a big Utah-based MLM company that, under the supervision of Dr. Tei-Fu Chen, sells health products mentioned in age-old manuscripts formerly owned by Chinese emperors—calls it "multiplication marketing" and, in one of its pamphlets, explains it this way:

> Would it surprise you to know that a penny deposited in an account that doubled every day, would grow to $1.28 in one week? By the end of the second week your original deposit would have grown to $163.84, and by the third week $20,971.52. Before you could say pick-up truck,

at the end of one month you would need one to haul your money home. One penny would have grown to $5,368,709.12 in just thirty days.

A mathematician would probably be less surprised by the size of those numbers than by the idea of a bank account that paid interest at an annual rate of 3,757,668,132,438,133,164, 623,168,954,862,939,243,801,092,078,253,311,793,131,665, 554,451,534,440,183,373,509,541,918,397,415,629,924,851, 095,961,500 percent.* But most people aren't mathematicians. The thought of watching a penny turn into more than five million bucks in thirty days is appealing in a way that preempts any application of logic. Having thus caught the reader's attention, Sunrider—like virtually all MLM companies—draws a conclusion that can't be drawn:

> Here's how it works. You share the Sunrider program and products with others, who in turn share the opportunity with more people. Before you know what is happening, you have hundreds of people marketing Sunrider products with all of their efforts contributing to your earnings and financial freedom.
>
> At Sunrider we call it sponsoring, and it is the principle of multiplication marketing upon which all wealth is built. Now instead of working for only eight hours a day, you are able to have a complete sales staff working hundreds of hours daily for your benefit and profit.

----
* In leap year, the interest rate would be 7,515,336,264,876, 266,329,246,337,909,725,878,487,602,184,156,506,623,586, 263,331,108,903,068,880,366,747,019,083,836,794,831,259, 849,702,191,923,100 percent. In any year, you'd need more than a pick-up truck to take your money home. Even if you withdrew it in $100 bills (the largest denomination now printed), the account would weigh more than the universe.

Multiplication marketing and Sunrider have proven that they work. All you need to do is substitute people for pennies and you will be well on your way to financial freedom and independence.

If you substituted people for pennies in the Sunrider example, you would surpass the population of the earth in less than five weeks. This is not a business for the faint-hearted.

As it happens, I am a Sunrider distributor. I became one by filling out a form and paying $24 for a sales kit. My sponsor is Robert Natiuk, who calls himself "the next Napoleon Hill" (Hill wrote *Think and Grow Rich*). Natiuk is co-author of *They Dared To Be Free*, a collection of MLM success stories, and a frequent contributor to *MLM News*, a monthly journal of the industry and the sponsor of Crossroads to Networking. Natiuk writes articles for *MLM News* in exchange for free advertising space. In one of his ads last year, he talked about his wife, Martha. "She looks a lot like Linda Evans of 'Dynasty' and loves our new luxury car, beach home, cruises—all made possible through SUNRIDER." The ad included a photograph of Natiuk (who does not look like John Forsythe) sitting in a tree, to drive home the point that many people feel "up a tree" with MLM.

I've never felt up a tree with MLM because I've never tried to sponsor any distributors. But if I did, here's what I'd probably do. First, I'd buy $100 worth of Sunrider products from Natiuk. My initial purchase might include Dandelion Root Concentrate, Loquat Syrup, Conco, Korean White Ginseng Concentrate, Siberian Ginseng Root Bark Concentrate, Metabalance 44, and several others. Making this purchase would enhance my body's powers of regeneration and move me up a rank in the Sunrider organization, from distributor

to trainer. I would now be entitled to a 5 percent commission
on any further purchases made directly by or through me.

Having done this, I'd call up my parents and ask them if
they'd like to become Sunrider distributors, too. Then I'd call
my wife's parents, my siblings, my wife's siblings, my barber,
the plumber, the guy at the hardware store, everybody in my
address book, and the entire staff of *The Atlantic*. If enough of
the people in my town seemed interested, I'd rent the gym at
the high school and, with Natiuk's guidance, hold a big introductory meeting. If I found myself sitting next to a fourteen-
year-old would-be juvenile delinquent smoking cigarettes in the
coffee shop of a hotel in Chicago, I'd recruit him. I also might
send around copies of a Sunrider videotape (each of which would
cost me $12) that explains everything about the program.

Let's say I did this for a while and managed to sign up
one distributor (my mom). My mom would now constitute my
"downline" in the Sunrider organization; Natiuk and everybody else on the direct path between me and Dr. Chen would
be my "upline." Of course, my mom would want to start building her own downline (which would also become part of my
downline, since I sponsored her). So she would become a
trainer by buying $100 worth of Sunrider products from me.
I'd get a 5 percent commission on this purchase.

This would be just the beginning. Full of enthusiasm, my
mom and I would start signing up other people like crazy.
Since my mom would be a trainer now, she wouldn't buy her
products from me anymore; she'd buy them directly from Sunrider. But that doesn't mean I'd stop getting rich. As soon as
the total purchases of my rapidly growing sales organization
exceeded $1,000, including $250 in the qualifying month, I'd
move up a rank to supervisor and my commission on my purchases from Sunrider would rise to 8 percent. In addition, I

would begin earning a special commission called an override on the purchases of all the people in my downline. A supervisor's override on downline trainer purchases is 3 percent.

At this point it begins to get a little confusing and, in truth, I don't understand how it works. But by increasing my organization's purchase totals from month to month I would begin to rise through the Sunrider ranks, from supervisor to manager to assistant director to director. A director is someone whose sales organization (his downline plus himself) has bought $8,000 worth of products (including $2,000 worth in the qualifying month). A director, according to a pamphlet in my sales kit, receives a 20 percent commission on direct purchases, a 5 percent override on purchases made by downline assistant directors and *their* downlines, a 9 percent override on purchases made by downline managers and *their* downlines, a 12 percent override on purchases made by downline supervisors and *their* downlines, and a 15 percent override on purchases made by downline trainers and *their* downlines.

Wait, there's more. There are five degrees of directorship: director, lead director, group director, master director, and executive director. As an executive director, I would earn director leadership bonuses of 7, 6, 5, 4, 3, 2, and 1 percent on various levels of directors below me. I would also receive a diamond pin, membership on the Executive Advisory Board, a one-week vacation for two anywhere in the world, and money from four separate profit-sharing plans. At some point along the way, I'd also have earned a free car or motorhome.

I forgot about retail sales. In addition to all those commissions, I'd be earning a retail markup of between 25 and 35 percent on sales outside my downline, assuming that I made any. I wouldn't have to share that money with anybody at all.

Retail sales are something of a sore point in the MLM

industry. Actually selling products to people outside one's sales organization is seldom given as much emphasis as signing up new distributors. At companies with minimum monthly purchase requirements ($100 worth at Sunrider), distributors sometimes simply buy what they have to in order to keep their commission checks coming. (At Sunrider, directors whose organizations' purchases fall below a certain level in any month also risk having parts of their downlines "rolled up" into their uplines and thus out of their commission streams.) Building a downline can be more profitable than actually hawking the product on the street. Many MLMers view retail selling as little more than a way to prospect for new distributors. The most sparsely attended seminar at Crossroads to Networking was the one on retail sales.

The stress on recruitment rather than selling is one aspect of MLM that perenially attracts the attention of government agencies. Companies that don't sell much to outsiders sometimes look like pyramid schemes. A pyramid scheme is like a lottery. It's a form of "multiplication marketing" in which participants contribute relatively small amounts of money to a pool in the hope of withdrawing relatively gargantuan amounts of money later, as more and more contributors are recruited. Most pyramid schemes are illegal (the world's largest pyramid scheme, the Social Security system, is not).

Recently, a non-MLM pyramid scheme known as "airplane" has turned up in states all across the country. In one version of the scam, people are invited to pay $1,500 in order to become one of eight passengers on an imaginary airplane with a crew of one pilot, two co-pilots, and four flight attendents. Once all eight passenger seats are filled, the pilot "bails out" with the money paid by the passengers—$12,000. Then the co-pilots become the pilots of two new airplanes, the flight attendants become co-pilots, and the passengers become flight attendants. Eight new paying passengers are recruited for each of the two new airplanes (providing new infusions of $12,000), and the game goes on.

If the world's supply of suckers were expanding exponentially, we could all get rich this way. As things are, the only way to make money in one of these schemes is to sign up very early, before the size of the money pool necessary to sustain it takes off for the stars.

Signing on early with a new MLM can pay off, too. Most new MLM companies go out of business very quickly. Distributors who build big downlines right away in such startups can often collect a few big commission checks before the company files for protection from its creditors. Wheeler-dealers known in the trade as "MLM junkies" often jump from one new company to another, trailing their downlines behind them. Distributors further down the money chain don't do as well; they can be left with a garage full of products they can't sell, or with a stack of worthless "product redemption certificates," or with nothing at all.

Executives of most MLM companies hate being discussed in the same breath with pyramid schemes, but in their company literature they often play up the pyramid angle themselves, as Sunrider does. Some MLM companies even illustrate their compensation plans with pyramid-shaped diagrams. One such company is Easyway Marketing, which is based in Schaumburg, Illinois. Easyway's compensation plan is called a three-by-nine matrix. The company sells grocery coupons, jewelry, and discounts on travel, prescription drugs, cars, and a variety of merchandise. Its introductory brochure is called "Your Guide to the Easy Life"; on the cover is a photograph of a silver-blue Mercedes.

None of this is meant to suggest that Sunrider, Easyway, or any other MLM company is necessarily breaking a law or defrauding its distributors. But their compensation plans, like those of virtually all MLM companies, are purposely designed to have a powerful appeal to the same combination of greed and gullibility that leads people to book $1,500 seats on imaginary airplanes.

*I*f you called up everybody in your downline and asked "Who's out to get MLM?" 67 percent would probably answer "the media." People in MLM are very suspicious of the press. It was this suspicion that led a good number of them to "Analyzing the Media and MLM," Clifton Jolley's seminar at Crossroads to Networking. Jolley got right to the point.

"How many of you are in MLM to make money?" he asked. Just about everybody in the room raised a hand, nodded, or grunted affirmatively. Then Jolley asked another question. "How many reporters do you suppose go into journalism to make money?" This produced a lot of chuckling. Reporters, as everyone knows, do what they do in order to emphasize the negative and make life miserable for other people.

"A good legal secretary makes more than a beginning journalist at *The New York Times*," Jolley went on. "The basic motivation of people who are affiliated with the press is very different from the motivation of the large majority of people in this room. That's the first thing you have to understand: that the point of view is remarkably removed from what you understand of the world."

Jolley was trying to explain why reporters sometimes seem to have it in for MLM. He's in a good position to know. He's a former communications professor who is now president of Avenues Communications, a consulting firm whose clients are mostly MLM companies. He writes a newspaper column in Salt Lake City's *Deseret News*, but this low-paying activity is merely an outlet for any remaining negativism that wealth-beyond-his-wildest-dreams has failed to purge from his system.

For the most part, I thought, Jolley's seminar was pretty good. He gave some sound advice about how to deal with reporters (don't lie to them, don't ask them when their stories will appear, don't wear a ten-thousand-dollar gold Rolex and sit on the hood of your Rolls-Royce when *Forbes* comes over to take your picture). But his comment about the salaries of reporters and legal secretaries made me pause.

I don't know what legal secretaries or *New York Times* reporters make, but I have some idea of what people in MLM make. According to Jeffrey Babener, a bright young MLM attorney who gave a seminar on legal issues with D. Jack Smith, the industry consists of somewhere between five million and ten million distributors who sell between $10 billion and $20 billion worth of products and services every year. Let's say there are ten million people doing $20 billion worth of business. That works out to $2,000 in gross sales per person per year. Subtract product cost, phone bills, car expenses, gymnasium rentals, and purchases made for personal use and there isn't very much left. The average MLM distributor, I would guess, can't be clearing more than fifty dollars a month. I like making up facts and ruining people's reputations as much as the next reporter, but if journalism didn't pay better than that, I'd do something else. And I'll bet there aren't more than a few dozen reporters at *The New York Times* who make less than six hundred dollars a year.

Does anybody in MLM make big money? Clearly some people do. There were some prosperous-looking consultants at Crossroads to Networking, and there are MLM executives who live in seven-million-dollar houses and fly around in private jets. Many companies publish glossy in-house magazines filled with pictures of happy distributors sitting on the hoods of their new luxury cars or yucking it up on company jaunts to island paradises. *MLM News* has a monthly feature called "Portrait of a Winner," a biographical sketch of someone making (or claiming to make) at least $100,000 a year. But the number of people who gross even a thousand dollars a month in MLM is very, very small. The great majority of MLMers could make a lot more money in a lot less time working behind the counter at MacDonald's.

Of course, nobody ever achieved financial freedom by working behind the counter at McDonald's. MLM is alluring because it seems to offer not a job but a means of transcending the economy altogether. But the appeal is an illusion. Those tantalizing compensation schedules actually work against virtually all distributors, whose sales efforts serve mostly to line the pockets of a small handful of other people.

People may sign up with MLM companies because they dream of getting rich, but most of the ones who stay do so for other reasons. One is that it makes them feel important. Receiving a commission check in the mail can be a transforming experience for someone who feels locked out of the mainstream economy, even if the check is only a rebate on a purchase he made himself. A man with a downline is a man who knows he isn't standing on the bottom rung. The standard MLM message is simple: If you're strong enough inside, if you're one of the few who are tough enough to stick it out, you'll be rich. When it doesn't work out that way, unsuccessful distributors often blame not the companies but their own characters.

There's also a heavy evangelical element in MLM. Successful MLM companies maintain their downlines by turning their distributors into crusaders. "People will work for money but they'll kill for a cause," someone said at Crossroads to Networking. One participant told me that MLM is "60-percent Christian"; he was referring to the Christianity of Jerry Falwell and Robert Schuller. Also of Brigham Young. Mormons are a big presence in MLM. The scarcity of alcohol at our hotel was not viewed as an inconvenience by most of the people in attendance. The symposium participant who attracted some of the most admiring attention from other participants was a man from Issaquah, Washington, who was starting an MLM company that would sell books, videos, gifts, and other items with a Christian theme.

*M*LM has been around since at least 1945, when a company called Nutrilite adopted a multilevel commission schedule for its line of nutritional supplements. Amway and Shaklee have been in business since the late 1950s. But a lot of people at Crossroads to Networking told me they thought MLM was just now entering its infancy as an industry. In the next few years, I was told, MLM is going to have a huge impact on the economy. Jeff Babener, the young attorney, told me that he thinks MLM distributor networks have an enormous potential. "More and more companies that are outside MLM are looking at this as a new forum, a new channel for marketing their products," he said in the legal seminar. MCI's success with Amway, he said, proves that MLM has economic muscle. He may be right.

I don't think he is, though. I had a very good time at Crossroads to Networking, and I met a lot of nice people, but the numbers don't add up. An MLM network is actually an inefficient mechanism for moving products through the economy. Starting an MLM company is cheap only because most of the overhead (warehousing, transportation, promotion) is absorbed by naïve distributors. Most MLM distributors don't even think of their own time as a cost of doing business; if they ever added up their expenses and computed their earnings as hourly wages, they'd be appalled. Also, because of the heavy commission schedules, introducing a truly new product through MLM is next to impossible. The industry depends instead on products that cost very little to develop and manufacture (vitamins, cosmetics, food supplements) or on services that have little actual value (discount travel clubs).

In the end, the words that stuck with me were those of Edwin L. Madison, a symposium participant and the president of a Texas-based company that sells scholarship information and provides other services for college applicants. Madison is a great big man who sounds a little like Lyndon Johnson. He had come to Crossroads to Networking because his sales force had been urging him to take the company MLM. Before one of the seminars, he turned around in his seat to talk to me.

"Statistics show that the average salesman works about fifty-eight hours a week but spends less than seven hours of that actually selling," he said. "My guys' theory is that multilevel will give them an easy way to prospect."

Before coming to Crossroads to Networking, Madison had been fairly certain that his company would move into MLM in the near future. Now he felt differently. "The thing that discourages me about MLM," he said, "is that we haven't been able to find anybody at this symposium who's been in business for as long as three years."

(1987)